THE RISE AND FALL
OF ITALIAN TERRORISM

NEW DIRECTIONS IN COMPARATIVE AND INTERNATIONAL POLITICS

Series Editors
Peter Merkl and Haruhiro Fukui

ABOUT THE BOOK AND AUTHORS

Between the late 1960s and the early 1980s Italy suffered one of the most severe waves of domestic political terrorism experienced by any Western democracy. During those years, Italian terrorists committed more than 12,000 acts of political violence. The 1978 assassination of former prime minister Aldo Moro and the 1980 bombing of the railroad station in Bologna, in particular, attracted world-wide publicity. Aside from its magnitude, Italian terrorism has been distinguished from that in other Western democracies by the fact that very little violence can be traced to the grievances of ethnic or religious minorities and by the prominent role of right-wing bands.

This book relates the formation, development, and eventual defeat of both neo-Fascist and left-wing terrorist groups in Italy. In addition to assessing the historical origins and contemporary manifestations of Italian terrorism, the authors examine the biographies of 2,500 individuals who participated in the violence, answering such questions as who the terrorists were, where they came from, and what led them to commit violent acts. The authors explore the causes of violence not only by reviewing terrorist groups' ideological pronouncements but also by analyzing the social, economic, and political conditions in those sections of Italy hardest hit by terrorism. Finally, the book describes the actions taken by the much-maligned Italian state to overcome successfully the terrorist threat.

Leonard Weinberg is professor of political science at the University of Nevada, Reno. **William Lee Eubank** is assistant professor of political science, also at the University of Nevada, Reno.

THE RISE AND FALL
OF ITALIAN TERRORISM

LEONARD WEINBERG
AND WILLIAM LEE EUBANK

WESTVIEW PRESS / BOULDER AND LONDON

Eubank would like to dedicate his portion of this effort
to his friends CM, CP, JMF, K^2 and Katrina

New Directions in Comparative and International Politics

This Westview softcover edition is printed on acid-free paper and bound in softcovers that carry the highest
rating of the National Association of State Textbook Administrators, in consultation with the Association
of American Publishers and the Book Manufacturers' Institute.

Copyright © 1987 by Westview Press, Inc.

Published in 1987 in the United States of America by Westview Press, Inc.; Frederick A. Praeger, Publisher;
5500 Central Avenue, Boulder, Colorado 80301

Library of Congress Cataloging-in-Publication Data
Weinberg, Leonard
    The rise and fall of Italian terrorism.
    (New directions in comparative and international
politics)
    Bibliography: p.
    Includes index.
    1. Terrorism—Italy—History—20th century.
2. Italy—Politics and government—20th century.
I. Eubank, William Lee. II. Title. III. Series.
HV6431.W44 1987 · 303.6′25′0945   87-14725
ISBN 0-8133-0541-1

Composition for this book originated with conversion of the authors' word-processor disks.

Printed and bound in the United States of America

The paper used in this publication meets the requirements of the American National Standard
for Permanence of Paper for Printed Library Materials Z39.48-1984.

6   5   4   3   2   1

CONTENTS

TABLES

ACKNOWLEDGMENTS

Much of the research on which this book is based was done in 1984 while I was a Fulbright Fellow at the University of Florence. The time spent in Italy offered me an opportunity not only to review the substantial body of writing about terrorism produced by both its observers and practitioners but also to obtain access to *sentenze* and other court documents concerning the operations of the major right- and left-wing terrorist groups. I also was able to interview police investigators, state prosecutors and judges in Florence, Turin, Milan and Rome—individuals who had first-hand experiences in the effort to repress terrorist activities. In many cases the sites of these encounters—criminal court buildings and regional police headquarters— told their own stories of public institutions under seige. The presence of heavily armed guards, metal detectors, closed-circuit television cameras and bullet-proof glass all testified to the atmosphere in which those who fought against the terrorists had done their work.

Among the large number of people in Italy who provided indispensable help in the completion of this project, some should be mentioned here. Those from the Italian system of justice were Patruno Nicola, Marcello De Roberto, Pier Luigi Vigna (Florence), Maurizio Laudi (Turin), Ferdinando Pomarici (Milan), Antonio Bacchiati (Rome). Scholars who offered their time and assistance were: Leonardo Morlino, Luigi Catnazaro, Luigi Bonante, Donatella della Porta, Franco Ferraresi and Gianfranco Pasquino. Among the American Embassy and consular officials, Frederic Vreeland (Rome), John Shippe (Florence) and Massimo De Leonardis (Milan) were particularly helpful. Cipriana Scelba, Luigi Filadoro and Maria Amata Basso of the Fulbright Commission deserve high praise. Special credit is due Sally Cantini, a teacher at the American School in Florence, for keeping my energetic son busy enough to allow his father to complete the work.

At the University of Nevada, Reno, Alison Trigero transposed the first version of the manuscript into a readable typescript. Don W. Driggs, Chair of the Department of Political Science and Sandra K. Neese, Director, Center for Applied Research, both provided critical last-minute institutional support to complete the final version of the book. Jackie Sharp, in our department, and G. Francis Smith, at the Center, both worked long hours in actually preparing this final version, and their extra effort at a critical time is much appreciated. Susan McEachern, Editor at Westview, should also be singled out for making this a pleasant experience and for her support. I would also like to thank my colleagues who put up with my, and Eubank's, work habits; their patience with idiosyncratic behavior is gratefully ac-knowledged.

Finally, and most importantly, my wife, Sinikka, should be recognized for the tolerance she has displayed in putting up with all of this.

Leonard Weinberg

1
INTRODUCTION

Italian democracy may not be as fragile as many of its observers feared or imagined. It has lasted more than twice as long as the Fascist dictatorship that preceded it. But the history of democratic rule in republican Italy is hardly like that of modern Switzerland or the Scandinavian countries. Since the end of the Second World War, Italy's citizens and their political leaders have had to overcome massive problems of both state and society that their counterparts in more tranquil parts of Europe have not encountered.

The particular problem to which this book is devoted is that of political terrorism. As a domestic problem, as opposed to an outgrowth of various international tensions, the recent experience of terrorism in Italy was among the most virulent and prolonged among the western democracies. The fact that it has largely been overcome should be a source of satisfaction for all those who regard the country and its people with affection. But the fact that it occurred in the first place and was so severe, raises troubling questions about the health of both the society and its democratic order. Our intent is to describe what happened and then seek to determine why thousands of Italians took up arms against their democracy.

To accomplish these tasks, the book has been organized in the following way. The second chapter provides an account of various theories, both conspiratorial and social scientific, that have been used to understand the violence. It also contains a commentary on the role of political terrorism and other forms of violence in Italian history since the country's unification in the 19th century.

Chapters three and four offer descriptions of the terrorist experience from its initiation at the end of the 1960s to its conclusion, or decline, in the 1982–83 period. The succeeding chapter identifies who the terrorists were, where they came from and what led them to embark on their violent careers. It is based on biographical information about more than 2,500 people who were identified as terrorists by newspaper accounts and court

1

records. This analysis is followed by an effort to explain their violent behavior not by reference to their abundant ideological pronouncements, but through an examination of the socio-economic, cultural and political milieu within which they committed more than 13,000 acts of violence. The sixth chapter examines what the widely criticized Italian state did to combat the terrorist threat with which it was confronted. The conclusion offers an interpretation of the impact political terrorism has had on Italy and the lessons that other democracies may derive from it.

Any book about terrorism, in Italy or elsewhere, should alert its readers about what its authors have in mind when they use the term. These days terrorism is a word that is commonly used to characterize a wide array of violent activities perpetrated by both private groups and governments. There is no commonly accepted definition of it, even among those who use it most frequently or study its manifestations most closely. One recent survey reports the use of 109 separable definitions in the period of 1936–1981.[1] We have no wish to add to this list. Despite the abundance, most definitions of terrorism currently in use stress the following properties.

First, terrorism involves activities in which the threat or use of violence is present. These activities—robberies, bombings, kidnappings, skyjackings, murders—are crimes under the domestic laws of the countries in which they are committed. Secondly, they are crimes committed not for reasons of private gain or personal vengeance but, instead, are politically motivated acts. Thirdly, the immediate victims of these politically inspired crimes usually are not their ultimate targets. Terrorism has a heavy psychological component. As the 19th century Russian anarchist Kropotkin put it: terrorism is propaganda by deed. It is a way of sending a message to a target audience in the hope that members of this audience will alter their behavior (e.g., become terrified and disoriented) in ways the perpetrators believe desirable. In short, terrorism is politically motivated crime intended to modify the behavior of an audience. Its immediate victims are used as instruments in the pursuit of this goal. And it is this kind of activity we have in mind when we use the word.

Outbreaks of terrorism, thus defined, may be either international or domestic. When terrorist groups, whose members are of one nationality, carry out attacks on foreign soil or on-board ships or planes belonging to another nation against victims of some third country (e.g., the Achille Lauro incident), we are confronted by an act of international terrorism. These are experiences then in which there is some nationality mix in the characteristics of their perpetrators, location, victims and target audience.

Domestic terrorism, on the other hand, refers to activities in which the requisite ingredients all belong to or are contained within one nation. The short-lived operations of the Symbionese Liberation Army in the United States with its abduction and "conversion" of heiress Patty Hearst, is illustrative. This book deals with a large-scale and protracted outbreak of domestic terrorism. It is concerned with terrorist violence in Italy committed by Italians against other Italians, the purpose of which was to influence the course of that country's political life.

Italy was hardly the only industrialized democracy to have suffered a wave of domestic terrorism over the last two decades. West Germany, Japan, Spain, Canada, France and the United States also went through such violent experiences. However, there were some very striking ways in which the Italian case differed from the others. For one, terrorism in Spain, Great Britain, Canada and even to a certain extent France and the United States, was stimulated by ethnic or separatist grievances. The causes of Basques in Spain, Catholics in Northern Ireland, Quebecois in Canada, Corsicans in France and Puerto Ricans in the United States were ones which terrorist groups in these countries sought to champion. But terrorism of this ethnic/separatist genre was largely missing from the Italian experience. Instead, the Italian groups with which this book is concerned committed their deeds not on behalf of minority religious or geographically concentrated ethnic communities, but in the name of certain ideas.

Like their Italian counterparts, terrorist groups in West Germany and Japan, as well as some in France and the United States, used violence in the pursuit of ideologically defined goals, ones based on equally ideological understandings of economic and political conditions prevailing in their countries and in the international realm. For the most part though, in the other democracies terrorism inspired by ideology was dominated by groups which professed their fidelity to the Marxist-Leninist revolutionary tradition. Also, not uncommonly, they were groups that defined themselves as part of an international struggle being waged against Western or American imperialism.

The Italian experience differs from the above in several ways. First, as we shall see, a good deal of Italian terrorism was inflicted by groups radically opposed to the revolutionary aims of Marxist-Leninist organizations. One of the most distinctive features of the Italian experience was the strength and intensity of neo-Fascist terrorism. In none of the other democracies did this kind of right-wing terrorism achieve the virulence it took on in Italy. But the differences do not end here.

Italy's left-wing revolutionary terrorists also differed from their peers. Most obviously, there were more of them. While membership in German, Japanese or American bands was miniscule, their Italian counterparts, notably the Red Brigades and Front Line, numbered their adherents and active supporters in the thousands. Further, the Italian revolutionary terrorists were rather more provincial than their counterparts in the other democracies. The former were less inclined to view themselves as part of a violent international struggle waged against NATO, international capitalism and

American imperialism. Although mention of these enemies was not missing from their public statements concerning who they were fighting against, their overwhelming interest was with the revolutionary transformation of their own society.

For all these reasons, Italian terrorism appears to have been less like that experienced by the other industrialized democracies and more like the sort of violence experienced in the 1970s by such fragile democracies as those of Argentina and Turkey, countries whose post–World War II histories have been marked by periods of military dictatorship. Indeed, terrorism in Argentina and Turkey led to the interruption of democratic rule and the seizure of power by the generals. Yet, what separated Italy from Argentina and Turkey was the absence of direct military intervention. Despite some temptations along these lines, Italy's democratic regime was preserved. There was no declaration of martial law, nor did the military stage a coup d'état.

Notes

1. For a discussion see Alex Schmid, *Political Terrorism* (New Brunswick, N.J.: Transaction Books, 1983).

THE CAUSES OF ITALIAN TERRORISM: CONSPIRACIES, CONFLICT AND HISTORY

2

On February 8, 1984, the Roman daily *La Repubblica*, one of Italy's liveliest newspapers, published the results of a public opinion survey it had commissioned. Among the questions posed to a national sample of Italians was one which asked them to indicate which event or events in the last 50 years of the country's collective experience would receive the most attention from future historians. Now the last 50 years of Italian history have hardly been uneventful. These years have seen the collapse of Fascist rule, the invasion of the country by foreign armies, the end of monarchy and the beginning of democratic government, economic reconstruction as well as a period of unprecedented economic growth, and the rise from clandestinity of the largest Communist party in the West, to mention only several of the most obvious examples. Yet despite the abundance of alternatives from which to choose, a substantial plurality of Italians selected the recent wave of political terrorism. Fascism, or its collapse, finished a distant second.[1]

It is, of course, impossible to say how well Italians in 1984 have forecast what is likely to be in the minds of historians decades or centuries in the future. What is possible to say is what was in the minds of those who were asked the question. Terrorism may or may not have the kind of impact respondents to the question believe it will, but it has certainly had an impact on them. Thus, we should ask ourselves: what has happened in Italy in recent years to leave such an impression on its citizens?

The period of political terrorism to which the respondents assigned such importance is often believed to have started in 1969 with the bombing of the National Agricultural Bank at Piazza Fontana in Milan and to have concluded, or at least subsided, with the arrest and subsequent prosecution of large numbers of terrorists after the liberation from his Red Brigades kidnappers of the American General James Dozier in 1982. During the period between these two events, terrorist organizations claiming inspiration from either anarchist, communist or neo-fascist doctrines, committed thousands of acts of violence; one estimate made in 1980 put the figure at more than 12,000.[2] At one time or another, each of the country's 94 provinces was the site of political violence, some of them—Turin, Milan, Rome, Padua—experienced especially high levels of violence.

These events resulted in hundreds of deaths, including that of a former prime minister, thousands injured, including a pope, and still more thousands in prison for having committed the violence. All this occurred in a country governed by a democratic political regime, no less and probably somewhat more democratic in 1982 than it was in 1969, with an advanced industrialized economy and having a population noted justifiably for its cultural sophistication and social tolerance. How could such events have occurred in a country like Italy?

Conspiracies

One often expressed and widely accepted type of response has involved the allegation of conspiracy. The conspiratorial interpretation given widest currency these days is one that identifies the Soviet Union along with some of its Warsaw Pact and Middle Eastern allies as responsible for promoting and sustaining the activities of the left-wing terrorist groups in Italy. This version of the conspiracy theory has found support along a wide spectrum of political opinion. The octogenarian former President of Italy, Sandro Pertini, a Socialist and hero of the anti-Fascist Resistance, appealed to the Soviet Union to stop supporting terrorism in his country.[3] The American journalist Claire Sterling, a long-time resident of Italy, wrote *The Terror Network*, a best-seller built around this perception.[4] And although neither Pertini nor Sterling would find the company politically congenial, spokesmen for the Italian Social Movement, Italy's neo-fascist political party, also have seen the Soviets behind the violence.[5]

These views, which among other things, minimize bitter disagreements within and conflicts between the major terrorist groups, have not gone uncontested. Luigi Bonante, a professor of international relations at the University of Turin, has argued that the Russians were unlikely to try to destabilize Italy because the consequences of such behavior, if successful, might be a rightist regime even less sympathetic to Soviet interests than the present one.[6] Pier Luigi Vigna and other of Italy's leading state prosecutors, individuals who devoted years to the investigation of terrorist groups, also evince skepticism. Many of them have concluded that the roots of Italian terrorism are to be found in the country's social and economic conditions rather than in the plans of the KGB.[7]

This judgment is not far from that of Patrizio Peci, a former member of the Strategic Direction of the Red Brigades (BR). In his autobiographical account of life inside the BR, Peci admits that the organization developed ties to other terrorist groups operating in Western Europe as well as with the PLO. But he denies that there existed any links with foreign intelligence agencies. Further, Peci argues there was no foreign interference concerning the BR's ideological, strategic or tactical decisions.[8]

The issue of foreign involvement was also taken up by a special committee of the Italian Parliament given the responsibility to investigate the kidnapping and subsequent assassination of former Prime Minister Aldo Moro in 1978. After accumulating information and hearing testimony over several years, the committee published its findings in 1983. They emphasize the conclusion that the terrorist groups were formed, developed and continued to be directed by Italians from beginning to end. This is not to say, however, that the BR, Front Line (PL) and others did not receive assistance from the outside. In particular, "there have been contacts and exchanges of experience, arms and refuges with other terrorist organizations. . . ."[9] Specific references are made to the German Red Army Faction and to the Palestinians. But over the crucial matter of efforts by foreign intelligence agencies to exert direct influence or manipulate the Italian groups, the findings are negative. The committee discovered that several attempts were made to exert such direct influence, but that the Italians were reluctant to become involved. They feared that the development of a direct relationship would compromise their independence and self-defined role as a revolutionary vanguard in Italian society.

The Soviet Union and its allies have not been the only foreign states accused of involvement in a conspiracy to promote terrorism in Italy. Some fingers have also been pointed at the United States. For instance, Eleanora Moro, the assassinated prime minister's widow, continues to believe that the United States played a role in the murder of her husband. Her accusation apparently is based on a conversation her late husband had in Washington with then Secretary of State Henry Kissinger. Members of the Moro family testified that the Christian Democratic leader had been threatened by Kissinger during a visit to Washington in 1974 in an effort to dissuade him from doing anything to promote the entry of the Communist party into the Italian coalition government.[10]

In the various commentaries in which a covert American involvement is alleged, the charge of complicity in the Moro case is unusual. Most writers who have sought to uncover an American directed conspiracy have called attention not to the BR, Moro's executioners, but to the activities of neo-fascist organizations. This version of the conspiracy theory, particularly attractive to writers on the left, has it that the American CIA provided funds for its Italian counterpart the Defense Information Service (SID).

Until its reorganization in the mid-1970s, the SID had a reputation for involvement in domestic politics, particularly right-wing politics. Leaders of the SID were said to have consulted with and channeled funds to major neo-fascist groups: the New Order, National Vanguard and National Front.[11] Given publicly expressed American concerns about the dangers of a growing Communist party in Italy, accusations about support for the intensely anti-communist neo-fascist groups were probably inevitable.

But the list of foreign nations alleged to have conspired against Italy does not stop with the superpowers. At various times during the 1970s, Greece, when it was run by the military, as well as Libya and Israel, have all been accused of seeking to manipulate the major terrorist groups in Italy.

The terrorists themselves were hardly immune to this conspiratorial line of reasoning. In a resolution of the BR's Strategic Direction published in 1978, Italy was defined as being in the grip of an international conspiracy. In this document the BR's theorists asserted that multinational corporations using such instruments as the Trilateral Commission, NATO and the European Economic Community, had conspired to transform the country into an Imperialist State of the Multinationals (which they abbreviated as SIM).[12] The resolution went on to describe how SIM had developed and refined techniques, including the construction of concentration camps (a reference to new maximum security prisons the government was building), for the repression of the working class victims of capitalist exploitation. Even the Italian Communist party, denounced as "revisionist" and "opportunist" by virtue of its advocacy of eurocommunism and related heresies, was assigned a role, albeit an auxiliary one, in the implementation of the multinationals' conspiracy against Italy.

So far in this account, our focus has been on international forces engaged in plotting Italy's downfall, variously defined. These conspiracy theories have in common the view that external agents initiated, for different reasons, plans to use violence as a means of transforming the Italian political regime. Several thoughts come to mind here. First, if we assume for the moment that one or even all of the external conspiracies were at work, an appropriate question to ask is, so what? It is conceivable that the Soviet Union or the United States, for example, might have had a strategic interest in destabilizing Sweden, Finland or Switzerland. Surely one can construct plausible reasons for such efforts. Why did not these nations experience the enormous volume of violence that Italy did? The answer would seem to be that the domestic social, economic and political conditions in these countries were such as to immunize them from outside attempts to promote terrorism. There are now several thousand Italian citizens imprisoned for having engaged in terrorist activities. Why were so many of the country's own citizens willing to take up arms in an attempt to overthrow their own government? The response compels us to look at factors at work within Italy rather than at plots hatched in foreign places.

To say this is not to deny that Italy has been the site of international terrorist activity in recent years. During the late 1960s and early 1970s terrorists from Arab nations used Italy as a *teatro* in which to stage a series of spectacular attacks on planes bound from Rome to Tel Aviv and other Middle Eastern destinations.[13] In the 1970s and 1980s diplomatic represen-tatives and other foreign nationals resident in Rome were assassinated by some of their domestic political opponents sent on killing missions from home countries. Italian Jews attending worship services were shot, with several fatalities, as they left Rome's main synagogue. The assailants were identified as Arabs seeking vengeance for Israel's offensive in Lebanon. Of course, the most dramatic incident of international terrorism to have occurred in Italy was the attempted assassination of the Pope, an act committed by a Turkish citizen, Mehmet Ali Agca, apparently with the help of Bulgarian authorities.[14] To be sure, these were all acts committed on Italian soil, but the issues involved, the perpetrators and most of their victims had little to do with the domestic Italian political scene. It is the latter which is the object of our interest.

When we return our attention to Italian political terrorism, that is, terrorist operations committed in Italy by Italian groups against purely Italian targets, and begin to search for causes, we are once again confronted by conspiracy theories. For in addition to those theories which allege the foreign origins of Italian terrorism, there are others which make the claim of conspiracy but see it as having been devised and executed by Italians.

Journalists, as well some politicians and magistrates, have seen domestic conspiracies behind neo-fascist terrorism. One version evolved in the af-termath of the Piazza Fontana bombing and given wide currency in the early 1970s was the Strategy of Tensions. According to the Strategy of Tensions argument, the Italian Social Movement (MSI), under the leadership of Giorgio Almirante, decided to exploit the explosion of worker and student protest in 1968 and 1969 by following a double course of action. On the surface, respectable-sounding MSI spokesmen would present themselves as advocates of law and order and defenders of a silent majority upset by the wave of mass protest visible in the streets of the major cities. Below the surface, these spokesmen had other things in mind.

Specifically, neo-fascist leaders were simultaneously committed to a policy of covertly promoting political violence. According to this argument, neo-fascist cadres acting on orders from above committed acts of terrorist violence, such as the Piazza Fontana bombing, which were disguised in such a way as to make it possible for the MSI's sympathizers among the police authorities to blame the left for these deeds. If a climate of fear and uncertainty could be sustained in this manner, with the leftist groups being blamed for the terror, the public might become so disturbed that it would be willing to tolerate a military coup d'état. If not exactly marching on Rome, the neo-fascists would come to power in the wake and with the connivance of Italy's military and police establishments.[15]

Early adherents to this conspiracy theory were inclined to believe that all the terrorism Italy was beginning to experience in the early 1970s was the work of neo-fascists. They claimed that not only openly neo-fascist groups like the New Order and National Vanguard were engaged in covert terrorist activities, but that leftist organizations, which professed to be inspired by anarchist or Communist principles, were secretly controlled and manipulated by the neo-fascists. Individual members of these groups whose backgrounds in leftist organizations could not be ignored easily were portrayed as dupes. Their groups had been penetrated by neo-fascist provocateurs who were now directing their operations to achieve rightist, not leftist, objectives.

In recent years, the Strategy of Tensions has been superseded by still another conspiracy theory concerning the origins of neo-fascist terrorism. This version differs from the earlier one in two ways. First, it is more limited in scope. It claims to explain the roots of neo-fascist terrorism; the behavior of the leftist groups is not covered. Secondly, there is a shift in the source of the conspiracy. Leaders of the MSI are no longer identified as the principal conspirators. In fact, in some instances they are portrayed as having been victimized by the conspiracy.

The masterminds behind this conspiracy were the heads of the once secret Masonic Lodge Propaganda Due (P2), its former leader Licio Gelli in particular.[16] This allegation has it that Gelli conspired with other members of P2 (the membership included prominent politicians and high-ranking military and police officers) to promote neo-fascist violence through the mid-1970s. The intent, as with the Strategy of Tensions, was to prepare the way for a coup d'état which would thwart the Communist party's (PCI) march towards power and participation in national government. A bungled coup, allegedly attempted in December 1970 by the late neo-fascist military hero Valerio Borghese and his National Front organizations, is said to have involved P2 members within the state apparatus. By 1975 however, Gelli and his lodge brothers are said to have switched tactics and committed themselves to a policy of manipulating the country's center and right-wing political parties within the context of a democratic regime.

If Gelli and the other leaders of P2 are suspected of being the conspirators behind neo-fascist terrorism, an equivalent role for the left-wing terrorist groups has been cast for a former professor of political philosophy at the University of Padua, Antonio Negri. Negri, a prolific author on the subject of revolutionary change in advanced capitalist societies, was formally charged on April 7, 1979 with organizing a conspiracy aimed at overthrowing the

Italian government.[17] The indictment portrayed Negri as the eminence grise, the covert director of leftist terrorism in Italy. Not only was he accused of inspiring the formation of terrorist groups from among the more militant members of two extraparliamentary movements, Worker Power and Collective Autonomy, with which he had been affiliated, but he was also defined as the mastermind behind the BR and a key strategist in their kidnapping and murder of Aldo Moro.[18]

Largely on the basis of testimony provided by a "penitent" terrorist, Carlo Fiorini, Negri was arrested, jailed and indicted on these charges—along with about half the members of the political science faculty at the University of Padua. The details of Negri's role in the promotion of leftist terrorism will be explored in later chapters; suffice to say at this stage of our inquiry that by the time Negri was actually brought to trial and sentenced in 1984 the list of charges against him was radically reduced and the allegation that he was the conspiratorial mastermind diluted.[19]

What should we make of the array of conspiracy theories just described? One reaction is that there may be something inherent in terrorist activities which per se invite conspiratorial interpretations. Bombs explode in unexpected places for no apparent reason. Trains carrying vacation-bound passengers are derailed. Seemingly innocuous pedestrians suddenly take revolvers from their pockets and kill an equally unexceptional looking magistrate while he is waiting to get on a public bus that would take him to work. Groups with names like Mussolini Action Squads or Nuclei of Armed Proletarians, or a hundred other labels, claim responsibility. Acts such as these, especially if they are repeated often enough and are accorded enough publicity, leave many with the impression that obscure forces must be at work. The public's need to understand these forces may lead to the adoption of conspiratorial interpretations.

Furthermore, it seems undeniable that unlike more spontaneous forms of political violence, terrorist activities require a certain amount of planning and coordination; put succinctly, as in the case of a bank robbery committed by a band of thieves, acts of group terrorism necessitate some kind of conspiratorial behavior prior to their execution. The questions, though, are: At what level is the conspiracy devised? And how broad a range of events and groups does it encompass?

Conspiracy theories are hardly unknown in the context of American politics, particularly extremist politics. As observers of the 'paranoid style' in American political history have noted, these interpretations have been articulated by a long list of groups, most commonly among those at the rightist fringes of American political life. At one time or another these groups have reported hair-raising stories of attempts by foreign based forces, Masons, Jesuits, Jews, Communists and Insiders, to subvert American society and assume control of its political institutions.[20] The most distinctive attribute of these theories has to do with their scope. Clearly they have been comprehensive perspectives. "The typical conspiracy theory extends in space: it is international in scope; it extends in time: it stretches back in time and promises to stretch ahead interminably."[21]

The only Italian conspiracy we have discussed that achieves the level of comprehensiveness associated with the American 'paranoid style' is that articulated by the BR's Strategic Direction with its allusion to the multi-nationals. For the most part, the other theories seem intermediate ones, standing somewhere between the low level and limited range designs necessary to plan and execute bank robberies, kidnappings and murders on a continuing basis in order to achieve general political objectives, and the all-encompassing demonological plot associated with the 'paranoid style.' Such intermediate conspiracy theories have not been entirely missing from the American political scene either, although they have rarely been associated with terrorist operations. Some examples that come to mind are 1) theories purporting to explain the provocative role of President Roosevelt in the events leading to Pearl Harbor and American entry into World War II, 2) the Watergate scandal, 3) the Koreagate scandal, and 4) conspiracies believed by some to have been involved in the assassinations of Presidents Lincoln and Kennedy as well as civil rights leader Martin Luther King. Unlike the Italian versions, these American conspiracies usually have not included schemes whose ends are the overthrow of the incumbent political regime.

Some of the American conspiracies have proven to be real, others false, some vastly exaggerated and still others left with the claims to their explanatory capacity unresolved. Leaving aside, for the moment, the degree of truth or falsity in the Italian conspiracies, one is struck by their ability to achieve a remarkably high level of acceptance among members of the country's political class and politically attentive public. Illustratively, for a period during the early 1970s, leaders of the Italian Communist party (PCI) were instructed to avoid spending their nights at home for fear of a roundup that would follow a coup d'état.

Explanations for the high credence given the conspiracy theories may rest with several features of Italian political life. In particular, Italy is a country with a long history of combinazioni, of political understandings reached by a small number of leaders acting in secret. It is also a nation where the level of personal trust in others and political trust in government is quite low. And it is, after all, a country with a substantial neo-fascist movement and a vast Communist party. If these features are placed in the context of the serious social and political strains the country has experienced in the last two decades, the ready acceptance of conspiratorial accounts becomes more plausible.

Finally, whether or not the conspiracy theories are true or false, the fact of their widespread acceptance has real, not imaginary, consequences. If

a variety of institutions. The list of poorly functioning or overloaded institutions runs the gamut, but analysts place special emphasis on conditions in Italy's prisons as well as its secondary schools and universities. The frustrations and injustices experienced by those encountering these institutions, brought on by their inability to adapt to modern circumstances, have been held accountable for promoting violent political reactions.

But it is the failures and deficiencies of the Italian political system which have yielded the most numerous as well as the most intensely argued explanations for terrorism. The most general political explanation questions the democratic character of the country's political culture. According to this account, Italy, like West Germany and Japan, its axis partners in the Second World War, has suffered a massive wave of ideologically motivated terrorism because of nonacceptance of the democratic rules of the game by the Italian population, or at least significant segments of it.[26]

This argument, first expressed by the political scientist Maurice Duverger, has been used to explain the differing levels of domestic terrorism between Italy and France. France, like Italy, experienced a major episode of student and worker protest in the late 1960s; yet France, unlike Italy, did not have a prolonged wave of terrorism in the aftermath. The reason for the difference, so the argument goes, is that democracy has taken root in France while it has not, or at least not to the same extent, in Italy.

Whatever the weaknesses of this account (for one thing it ignores the somewhat less than democratic circumstances which led to General de Gaulle's return to power and the advent of the Fifth Republic), it nevertheless raises an important question about how Italians feel about their democratic political system. In this connection, studies of Italian public opinion conducted over the course of the 60s and 70s reveal a population with some very profound doubts about the effectiveness of this system.[27] From a figure of 8.5% in 1967 to 43.8% in 1980, the percentage of Italians reporting feelings of profound dissatisfaction with the functioning of their political system grew dramatically. Of course, it is true that the level of trust and confidence the American as well as other Western publics displayed in their democratic institutions also declined during this interval. But dissatisfaction is one thing, revolution something else. And in this regard, the Italian studies disclose the existence of a not insignificant minority of the population which believed that the system would only be changed by means of revolution (see Table 2.1). This revolutionary minority did not constitute an 'armed party' necessarily—judgments about what is required to achieve revolutionary change differ, and during the 1970s less than 2% of Italians expressed a willingness to use violence against people in order to achieve such change— it nonetheless points towards a rather obvious conclusion. There existed in Italy during this period not a revolutionary situation, but a terrorist situation, a situation in which several million people thought revolutionary

TABLE 2.1
Percentage of Italians Believing Their Political System Could Only
Be Changed by Revolutionary Means

	1970	1976	1978	1980	1982
Percent of Italians Believing in Revolution To Achieve Change in System	8	13	9	6	7

Source: Giovanna Guidorossi, Gli Italiani e la politica (Milan: Franco Angelli Ediotre, 1984) p.61.

change necessary and several hundred thousand evidently endorsed the desirability of anti-person violence to achieve it. But this judgment must be viewed against the vast majority of Italians who, satisfied or dissatisfied with the political system, endorsed neither revolution nor violence. The question which should be asked now is: What properties does the Italian political system exhibit that would have given rise to a terrorist situation? One response assigns blame to the Christian Democratic party's (DC) domination of national political life. Proponents of this explanation refer to Italy as having a 'blocked' political system. The country was susceptible to terrorism because efforts to achieve social, economic and political reforms confronted an insurmountable barrier. This blockage refers to two related system characteristics. The first one is the hegemonial role in politics played by the DC with its seemingly perpetual hold on the levers of power in the system, a hold only partially relinquished when the party had to abandon the prime ministership in 1981.

The second characteristic of the blocked system has to do with the policy consequences of DC rule. Attempts by some of the DC's government coalition partners, notably the Socialists, to initiate meaningful reforms were delayed, diluted or prevented by DC opposition. As a result the reformist aspirations of center-left coalition governments during the 1960s and 1970s, Christian Democratic–Socialist alliances with the participation of small center parties, waned the longer the coalition endured.[28] The effect of the blocked system, its hypothesized relationship to the terrorist phenomenon, was that it left a significant minority of Italians with the impression that change could not be accomplished within the context of the existing rules of the game.

A seemingly obvious pole of attraction for this segment of the population was the Communist party. But the Communists themselves were undergoing changes that proved equally frustrating to the country's professedly revolutionary minority.

In the late 1960s and early 1970s the PCI, under the leadership of party secretaries Luigi Longo and Enrico Berlinguer, was in the process of re-emphasizing its adherence to the principles of democratic government and rallying its vast membership behind the banner of eurocommunism. This process was exemplified, in 1974, by Berlinguer's advocacy of an 'historic compromise' with the Christian Democrats and the Socialists, a compromise intended to bring the PCI into a national coalition government. Among other things, the proposal was a device by which the party hoped to extend its electoral appeal to wider elements of the middle class. Unsympathetic journalists and politicians on the right expressed skepticism about the authenticity of the PCI's democratization. Strained comparisons were made between the historic compromise initiative and the situation in Eastern Europe after World War II when the Communists quickly converted their presence in coalition cabinets into monopoly control over state power.

If conservatives were doubtful and searched for hair-raising analogies, the PCI's left-wing critics were not.[29] From their perspective, the Communists, after decades of struggle against capitalism involving the use of the Marxist-Leninist vocabulary and attendant revolutionary symbolism if not action, had abandoned their historic mission. Instead the party had embarked on a policy of strengthening the capitalist system. As these critics saw it, the PCI was in the process of becoming a social democratic party. The desire to achieve legitimacy as a democratic force meant the Communists were becoming bourgeois reformers; they had become opportunists abandoning the working class in search of support among class enemies.

The linkage between PCI policy in these years and the growth of left-wing terrorism is a complex one which may be viewed from a variety of perspectives. From one such viewpoint, the conflict between the Communists, their leftist critics and the left-wing terrorists, who also claimed to be acting within a Marxist-Leninist framework, represented the continuation of a dispute between maximalism and reformism that can be traced back to the earliest years of the socialist movement in Italy. Suffice to say at this stage of the analysis, the period during which the terrorist groups were being formed was one in which the PCI was being viewed by many on the left as no longer seriously committed to the kind of comprehensive changes that those who engaged in mass protest in 1968 and 1969 believed necessary.

A review of the political explanations for Italian terrorism would be incomplete without reference to the central role played by the neo-fascist movement. This role was played in two ways, one passive and the other active. Passively, the very presence of a large neo-fascist movement in Italian political life served as a provocation to leftist groups whose adherents' view of the world was shaped in no small measure by stories of the heroic struggle waged by the Resistance against Fascist rule during World War II. The provocative role played by neo-fascism in stimulating leftist terrorism was heightened by the abundance of press accounts of neo-fascist violence, para-military camps and conspiracies published in the late 1960s and early 1970s.

Insofar as the active component of its role is concerned, the events of these crucial years of mass protest produced a revitalization of neo-fascism. Control of the MSI passed from the hands of conservatives committed to a failed policy of gradually joining a rightist alliance with monarchists, Liberals and Christian Democrats, into those of men like Giorgio Almirante, its new secretary, and Giuseppe "Pino" Rauti, a long time leader of the extra-parliamentary and anti-democratic New Order movement, whose motto ("Duty is Our Honor") and insignia, borrowed from the Nazi SS, were reflections of the movement's outlook on democratic politics.[30] If leftists saw in the neo-fascist presence a provocation, the neo-fascists themselves saw an opportunity. The opportunity was based on the exploitation of popular fears of the mass protests going on in schools, universities and industrial plants all over northern Italy. And if young leftists dreamed of the anti-fascist Resistance, the neo-fascists dreamed of the period after World War I when the reaction to Red insurgency led to the advent of the original fascist regime.

To this point in our review of explanations for terrorism, we have discussed accounts which focus on the broad forces at work in Italian society and polity which contributed to the development of a climate conducive to terrorist violence. Let us now turn our attention to accounts which use this climate as background but which emphasize the importance of the actors themselves in understanding the phenomenon.

As in other countries subject to widespread terrorist activities as opposed to occasional acts of individual assassination, explanations based on the alleged psychopathological traits of individual terrorists have not achieved much acceptance in the Italian context. On occasion the behavior of certain individual terrorists, such as the neo-fascist Mario Tuti, a draftsman from Empoli who murdered two policemen, has led to claims of mental illness, but these instances have been the exceptions not the rule. In general, the biographical information concerning the members of terrorist bands has stressed the normality of their family backgrounds and other social affiliations.[31]

Some attempts to explain terrorism by reference to the backgrounds of individual terrorists have examined the political and religious orientations of their families. These efforts may be summarized by the neologism 'Cattocomunismo'.[32] This word is used to indicate that many of the early leaders of left-wing terrorist groups, the BR and Nuclei or Armed Proletarians (NAP) especially, came from either Catholic or Communist families. These backgrounds, in turn, are held responsible for stimulating an outlook of unfulfilled idealism with the offspring seeking to put into practice, through violence, the principles they acquired in childhood. While it cannot be denied that individuals like Renato Curcio and Alberto Franceschini of the BR's 'historic nucleus' came from such backgrounds, the discovery of this pattern does not take us very far. In a country where a sizable majority of the population is Catholic and a substantial minority is of Communist persuasion, the discovery that the families of terrorists were much like the rest of the country does not constitute a compelling explanation.

More successful attempts to account for the development of terrorism are ones that refer to the 'culture of 1968' and the formation of extra-parliamentary political movements. Here the focus is shifted from the background of the individual terrorist to the origins of the terrorist organizations. These accounts emphasize the importance of the mass student and work turmoil of 1968-69 and the concomitant formation of several revolutionary New Left political movements.[33] The revolutionary goals of these movements were to be achieved through the mobilization of student-worker alliances and of continuous mass agitation and protest. Over the course of the 1970s and particularly as the result of an unexpected DC electoral success in 1976 along with a corresponding rejection by the electorate of New Left appeals, these movements deteriorated. The likelihood of their being able to achieve their goals became progressively more remote, a shocking discovery to those whose expectations of revolutionary change had been raised by the events of 1968-69.[34] And it was in the wake of the collapse of the New Left movements that the terrorist groups were formed, and it was from these movements that the groups were able to recruit a significant proportion of their members.

The events of 1968-69 also had an impact on the formation of new and the revitalization of previously organized neo-fascist groups. Several studies report a list of more than 60 such groups that formed in the years immediately following the explosion of mass protest.[35] Young men angered by the leftist protests and what they seemed to portend for the future gathered in certain squares in Milan and at street corners in certain neighborhoods of Rome to mobilize for violent counterattacks against the New Left movements. Some passed through periods in the MSI's youth organizations, others spent their summers at para-military training camps at sites along the Italian peninsula; all were animated by a need to confront the leftist revolutionaries.

Terrorism in Italian History

The foregoing efforts to explain political terrorism have in common the fact that they seek to account for the growth of the phenomenon by linking it to relatively short-term fluctuations in Italian society and polity; they review changes close in time to the violent events themselves. These events and their proximate causes are seen rather like a storm cloud in an otherwise blue sky. But such a picture is a highly distorted one. It ignores the fact that the history of political terrorism in Italy is virtually as long as that of the country's experience as a unified nation state.

In fact, political violence in general has been a common feature of Italian public life since the achievement of national unification. With the exception of the 21 year rule of Fascist dictatorship (1922–1943), Italian history, before and after Mussolini, has been characterized by an enormous volume of political violence. Historians record major violent events as occurring at a pace of about one every two years from the 1860s until the advent of Fascist rule and then resuming at only a slightly reduced rate in the years following World War II.[36] Much of this violent activity arose in connection with worker and peasant strikes, land seizures and factory occupations. But there were also bread riots, anti-tax riots and anti-war protests. Some events involved attacks against government authorities; other conflicts involved disputes between private groups.

These instances of collective violence do not fit the definition of political terrorism. They were relatively spontaneous and large-scale expressions of economic and political discontent. Terrorism is something else.

The first displays of political terrorism in modern Italy began in the 1870s and were encouraged by the newly formed Anarchist Federation, an organization inspired by the writing and presence of the Russian Bakunin. In that decade as in the present era, the Italian public was encouraged to believe that acts of revolutionary terrorism were the work of forces external to Italy; the anarchists, members of the First International, were identified as part of a secret international revolutionary force.[37] Anarchist violence seems to have been motivated by two objectives. First, there was the desire, as in the attempt in the summer of 1874 to seize the city of Bologna, to inspire others. As the anarchist leader Malatesta wrote: "The Italian Federation believes that the insurrectionary deed . . . is the most efficacious means of propaganda."[38] But in addition to this expression of classic terrorist logic, there was also the intent to take revenge against individual symbols of state authority in circumstances where the state acted to repress worker organizations and persecute their spokesmen.

To illustrate, during the 30 year period between the Italian government's conquest of Rome in 1870 and the beginning of the 20th century, individuals or small groups of anarchists attempted to assassinate the king on several occasions. Bombs were thrown during patriotic processions in Florence, Pisa and Naples. In other cases, individuals sought to commit regicide by using knives and hand-guns. Nor were the activities of Italian anarchists confined to Italy. In 1894 the president of France was assassinated by a young Italian anarchist, an act which provoked outbreaks of anti-Italian violence in several French cities. The Spanish prime minister likewise was killed by another Italian anarchist as was the Empress of Austria-Hungary.

Finally, in the summer of 1900, Italy's own monarch Umberto was assassinated in Monza by Gaetano Bresci, an emigré to the United States who had joined an anarchist circle in Paterson, New Jersey, and then returned to Italy to commit the deed.

These acts of anarchist terrorism produced responses with a distinctly contemporary ring to them. The acts themselves tended to occur in the midst or in the aftermath of bouts of mass protest. They were met by the enactment of special legislation by authorities who used the events to portray all leftists, republicans, socialists as well as anarchists, as part of a single conspiracy. The pro-government press sought to stimulate patriotic and anti-revolutionary reactions. Social scientists used their methodologies to "prove" that anarchists were mentally ill or common delinquents without authentic political convictions. Leaders of Italy's hard-pressed leftist organizations issued statements disavowing responsibility and condemning the killings. Allegations were made that police spies were used as agents provocateur.[39]

Despite adverse public reactions, anarchists continued to commit terrorist acts during the first decades of the 20th century, though their targets became less exalted than kings, presidents and empresses. For instance, an anarchist attacked an army officer in front of La Scala in 1904 as a protest against Italian militarism. And most spectacular of all, in March 1921 three anarchists were arrested for having set off a bomb at the Diana theatre in Milan; the resulting explosion killed close to two dozen people.

As is true with so much of the phenomenon, opinions about the character of fascist violence differ. The facts are not in dispute. In the years preceding Mussolini's assumption of power in the fall of 1922, Fascist squads in central and northern Italy employed massive doses of violence to intimidate and repress the Duce's left-wing and putatively revolutionary opponents.[40] Was this terrorism? The Fascist philosopher Sergio Panunzio thought it was not. Panunzio based his argument on the distinction between force and violence. He reasoned that force, like the defensive character of a just war in Catholic theology, was obedience to necessity. The only alternative for those who employed force was suicide. They were attacked and therefore confronted by the necessity of either defending themselves or perishing. Violence, on the other hand, was a voluntary activity. Those who used it, i.e., revolutionaries, decided when or if to attack the social and political order.[41] For Panunzio it seemed clear that worker and peasant organizations in post-war Italy had engaged in the voluntary use of violence to promote revolutionary change while the Fascists *squadristi* had done nothing more than defend themselves and their country by the legitimate use of force. They had no alternative. If we adopt Panunzio's argument and identify terrorism as a voluntary activity, then Fascist behavior escapes the definition.

But Panunzio's writing is hardly the last word on the subject. The contemporary writer Carlo Marletti sees Fascist Squadrism as having been different than anarchist terrorism but terrorism nonetheless. From this perspective, Fascist behavior represented a significant departure from that of the anarchists. For one thing, the style of Fascist squadrism was original. There was a quality of play and theatricality, a need to humiliate and make its victims appear ridiculous, that was missing from the anarchist attacks. Thus, Fascist violence was characterized by a kind of gratuitous cruelty. Furthermore, the Fascist squads were the first terrorist groups in Italy to break down the distinction in selecting victims between clearly defined enemies, socialists or anti-fascists, and individuals belonging to suspect social categories, workers and peasants. And crucially, from the point of view of our earlier definition of terrorism, Fascist violence had the effect of promoting a numbing and diffuse sense of fear intended to silence those who observed it.[42]

Whatever else one may say about either revolutionary anarchist or Fascist violence, political terrorism did not cease with Mussolini's conquest of state power. Unlike the phenomenon of collective or mass violence, the Fascist dictatorship did not prevent the occurrence of terrorist events. Indeed the Fascist regime also promoted the use of terrorism as a way of dealing with its enemies.

The most notorious episode of Fascist terrorism during Mussolini's rule was the abduction and assassination of the social democratic deputy Giacomo Matteotti. After Matteotti had protested against the widespread use of intimidation by the Fascists at the 1924 elections, Mussolini encouraged members of a Fascist gang to silence his opponent.[43] Although Matteotti's murder was the most dramatic act of its kind committed during the Fascist era, it was far from the only one. Nor was Fascist violence confined to Italy. Enemies of Mussolini who had taken refuge abroad also were attacked. Thus the leaders of the exiled anti-Fascist *Giustizia e Libertà* movement, Carlo and Nello Rosselli, were killed in 1937 by French fascists acting on orders from Rome.[44] Further, the Fascist dictator sought to export terrorism in order to destabilize political regimes in other countries, notably Yugoslavia. In an attempt to dismember this neighboring country, Mussolini provided support, including terrorist training camps in Italy, to Croat nationalists who hoped to create a separate state of their own. In 1934 members of this group assassinated King Alexander of Yugoslavia along with the French Foreign Minister in Marseilles. French authorities discovered that some of the Croat murderers were carrying passports and money furnished in Italy. Despite French protests, Mussolini denied any Italian responsibility. In light of contemporary accusations that other nations have sought to destabilize Italy by supporting terrorist groups, this episode conveys a certain irony.

Mussolini and other Fascists were not only promoters of terrorist violence, they were also its targets. The Duce was the object of at least four assassination attempts, the last of which reportedly occurred in 1926 and was used as an excuse to justify the elimination by law of the political opposition. Historians believe that on some occasions these attacks were encouraged by agents provocateur; certainly their occurrence was exploited by the Fascist regime for its own purposes.[45] Nonetheless, two of the attempts were committed by individuals with anarchist backgrounds and a third by a Socialist deputy.

In terms of the damage done, the worst single terrorist event during the Fascist era was a bombing in Milan in 1928. On April 12 as the King arrived to inaugurate the *Fiera Campionaria* a bomb exploded in the crowded square which killed 18 people and left 40 more injured. The Communists were blamed. Although the *Fiera Campionaria* bombing was the worst act of its kind, it was hardly the only one. In 1932 bombs were set-off in Bologna, Turin, Genoa and Milan. A young Genovese anarchist was held responsible. A year later, and apparently in protest against the Church's reconciliation with the Fascist regime, another bomb was exploded, this time in St. Peter's Square. Four individuals on Holy Year pilgrimages were injured.

Just as Fascist violence directed against the regime's opponents was not limited to Italy, so too Mussolini's enemies engaged in direct action abroad. Accordingly, anarchists and revolutionary socialists killed a dozen Italian consular officials during the 1930s.

If the Fascist era began with a large dose of terrorist violence, that of the *Squadristi*, the end of Fascism likewise involved a substantial amount of terrorist activity. The context for its expression was the Italian Resistance movement. After Italy's capitulation to the Allies in 1943 and the ensuing German occupation of the country, an armed resistance movement was organized. In central and northern Italy, Resistance units engaged in guerrilla operations against the Nazis and supporters of the Italian Social Republic, the new Fascist regime Mussolini directed from the north. Militarily much of the Resistance consisted of rural-based hit and run attacks against Axis forces. Some of it involved risings in the major cities about to be liberated by British or American troops. Nonetheless, terrorism, as we have defined it, played a not insignificant role.

In Rome, Turin, Milan, Genoa, Bologna, Padova, Florence and other cities, small units organized under the name Patriotic Action Groups (GAP) committed a long list of terrorist acts. Under the overall direction of the Communist Garibaldi Brigades, these *Gappisti* assassinated Fascist party members and military officers as well as representatives of the German occupation authorities. The most illustrious of GAP victims was the elderly Fascist philosopher Giovanni Gentile, gunned down in front of his home in Florence.[46] In response to the wave of GAP bombings and assassinations, Mussolini sought to recapture the spirit of 1921 by ordering the commanders of his anti-partisan Black Brigades to take reprisals against those suspected of aiding the *Gappisti*, as well as against totally innocent civilians who happened to be in the wrong place at the wrong time.[47] Vengeance of this type was precisely what the GAP leaders hoped to induce. Their objective was to transform the indifferent into anti-Fascist and potentially revolutionary masses. They expected Black Brigades and Nazi reprisals would have this effect.

The end of the Second World War did not produce a revolution in Italy. It did, however, leave the country with a residue of political terrorism, inspired by anarchist, Fascist and Communist doctrines, as well as some scores to be settled by the adherents of these doctrines. And although the end of the war brought the Fascist era to its logical conclusion, it did not bring an end to political terrorism in the country.

In the months immediately after the war, bands of ex-partisans carried out acts of vigilante justice against their former fascist tormenters. For example, on the evening of July 6, 1945 a group of former Resistance fighters entered a prison near Vicenza, held a summary trial and then executed 53 fascist prisoners.[48] Estimates vary on the number of former fascist officials killed in this manner. The figure later announced by the government was 1,750 dead.

Reconstructed neo-fascist groups over the next several years sought to make their presence felt by attempting various acts of terrorism. One band took over a radio station in Rome and forced its employees to play *Giovanezza*, the Fascist anthem. Another group tried unsuccessfully to plant explosives aboard an Italian Navy ship that was going to be turned over to the Soviet Union as reparation.[49] The most dangerous act of neo-fascist terrorism in the postwar period was the attempted assassination of Communist leader Palmiro Togliatti, an event that almost set-off a mass insurrection. Togliatti was shot on July 14, 1948 by a neo-fascist youth as he was leaving the Chamber of Deputies in Rome.[50] For the next several days, prefects in the northern cities reported Communist workers occupying plants and ex-partisans of the Garibaldi Brigades taking up arms. The PCI leadership succeeded in persuading their followers of the fruitlessness of an attempt at revolution. Nonetheless, it was a close call.

The 1950s and early 1960s were not free of political violence either; much of it though was the sort of collective violence described earlier, and involved worker responses to police restrictions on their protests and manifestations. Some of it though exhibited the characteristics of terrorism: for example, the violent campaign waged by an underground group of German-speaking Italian citizens in the northern region of Trentino-Alto

Adige to detach the South Tyrol from Italian control and return it to
Austria.

In addition to these episodes, youth groups affiliated with neo-fascist
MSI committed a large number of acts of political violence that were neither
spontaneous reactions to police crackdowns nor, strictly speaking, exhibitions
of political terrorism. A partial list of these events includes the following:

Violent Acts Committed by *Neo-Fascist Youth Groups*	*Dates*
Attack on Rome offices of *Unita* newspaper	March 1953
Attack and vandalize Milan offices of *Unita* and *Avanti*	November 1953
Attack on local section of Communist party in Rome	January 1954
Attack on Palermo office of *Unita*	July 1954
Vandalize an art exhibition devoted to the Resistance in Rome	September 1954
Destruction of Two Communist section offices in Rome	September 1954
Throw incendiary at the *Rinascita* (Communist) bookstore in Rome	March 1955
Attempt to set fire to local Communist party office in Rome	March 1955
Attack on peasant cooperative in province of Rovigo	March 1955
Fire shots at home of ex-mayor of town in province of Rovigo	March 1955
Throw bomb at Communist federation office in Reggio Emilia	March 1955
Attempt to dynamite the offices of several political parties as well as archbishop's residence in Milan	January 1956
Attack on CGIL (labor federation) office in Rome	February 1956
Throw molotov cocktails at local Communist party office in Genoa	November 1956

Throw bomb at local Communist party office in Turin	February 1957
Detonate bomb in front of Resistance veterans' organization office in Rome	April 1957
Vandalize Communist party office in Trento	January 1959
Throw incendiary in hall of building where city council is meeting in Trieste (as protest against decision to allow instruction in Slovenian language in schools)	February 1959
Throw molotov cocktails at Casa Del Popolo in Milan	March 1959
Vandalize offices of Radical party in Milan	June 1960
Vandalize Socialist and Communist party offices in Bari	October 1960
Throw explosive inside office of Camera del Lavora in Perugia	February 1961
Set-off smoke bomb during performance of an anti-Franco Spanish film at theatre in Milan	February 1961

Though most of these events do not constitute political terrorism they do represent a form of small-scale, planned and covertly executed attacks from which neo-fascist terrorists in the late 1960s and thereafter could derive useful lessons.[51]

The foregoing account of the history of political terrorism in Italy has been intended to qualify explanations for the dramatic growth of the phenomenon in the country's recent political experience. As we have seen, these explanations have tended to emphasize the proximate social, economic and political circumstances that facilitated the development of a severe terrorist situation.

No doubt it would be an exaggeration to argue that since terrorism has been a relatively continuous feature in Italian politics since unification, thereby constituting the norm, what really should be explained are occasional interludes of peace and tranquillity, periods which represent deviations from the norm. This judgment is an exaggeration because political terrorism reached unprecedented levels, measured in intensity and by volume, from the late 1960s through the early 1980s. What the reader should bear in mind is that the tactics and behaviors labeled political terrorism became part of the repertoire of actions left and right wing political groups acquired as they sought to achieve their goals. Italian history made political terrorism available as a set of concrete and easily communicated events to ideologically sensitive and historically self-conscious groups, some of whom reacted to contemporary strains in the social and political order by invoking memories of the past.

Notes

1. *La Repubblica* (February 8, 1984), p. 7.

2. Mauro Galleni (ed.), *Rapporto sul terrorismo* (Milan: Rizzoli editore, 1981), p. 49.

3. *La Repubblica* (January 26, 1981), p. 1.

4. Claire Sterling, *The Terror Network* (New York: Holt, Rinehart & Winston, 1981).

5. See, for example, the minority report submitted by Franco Franchi and Michele Marchio to the parliamentary commission that investigated the kidnapping and assassination of Aldo Moro; *Relazioni di minoranza della commissione parlamentare d'inchiesta sulla strage di via Fani sul sequestro e l'assassino di Aldo Moro e sul terrorismo in Italia* (Rome: Tipografia del Senato, 1983) pp. 63–396.

6. Luigi Bonante (ed.), *Dimensioni del terrorismo politico* (Milan: Angelli editore, 1979).

7. Author's interview with Dott. Pier Luigi Vigna, Sostituto procuratore della repubblica, Florence, April, 1984.

8. Giordano Bruno Guerri (ed.), *Patrizio Peci: io l'infame* (Milan: Arnaldo Mondadori editore, 1983) pp. 171–172.

9. Senato della Repubblica, Camera dei Deputati, VIII Legislatura, *Relazione della commissione parlamentare d'inchiesta sulla strage di via Fani sul sequestro e l'assassino di Aldo Moro e sul terrorismo in Italia* (Rome: Tipografia del Senato, 1983) p. 151.

10. Ibid., pp. 19–22. On Signora Moro's present state of mind, author's interview with Frederick Vreeland, political counselor, at the U.S. Embassy in Rome, June, 1984.

11. See for example, Renzo Vanni, *Trent'anni di regime bianco* (Pisa: Giardini editori, 1976) pp. 149–158.

12. This document is reproduced in Giorgio Bocca (ed.), *Moro: una tragedia italiana* (Milan: Bompiani, 1978) pp. 49–111.

13. Luigi Migliorino, "L'Italia e il terrorismo internazionale," in Bonante (ed.) *op. cit.* pp. 313–346.

14. Claire Sterling, *The Time of The Assassins* (New York: Holt, Rinehart & Winston, 1983).

15. See for example, Daniele Barbieri, *Agenda nera: trent'anni di neofascismo in Italia* (Rome: Coines edizioni, 1976) pp. 145–184; Marco Fini and Andrea Barberi, *Valpreda: processo al processo* (Milan: Feltrinelli, 1974) pp. 90–105.

16. Tina Anselmi, *Il complotto di Licio Gelli: relazione di Tina Anselmi, presidente della commissione parlamentare sulla P2*, reprinted as a special supplemental in *L'Espresso* (May 20, 1984).

17. For a sample of Negri's writing see *Proletari e stato* (Milan: Feltrinelli, 1976), and *Crisi e organizzazione operaia* (Milan: Feltrinelli, 1974).

18. For one of the indictments see, Francesco Amato, Giudice Istruttore, *Ordinanza/Sentenza* N10067/79, Tribunale di Roma, Ufficio Istruzione, pp. 61–209. For a history of the case see Giancarlo Scarpari, "La vicenda del '7 aprile'" in Magistrature Democratica (eds.), *La Magistratura di fronte al terrorismo e all' eversione di sinistra* (Milan: Franco Angelli editore, 1982) pp. 37–63.

19. Daniele Mastrogiacomo, "Autonomia, 7 secoli di carcere," *La Repubblica* (April 16, 1984) p. 5.

20. Richard Hofstadter, *The Paranoid Style in American Politics* (New York: Vintage Books, 1967) pp. 3–40; Seymour Martin Lipset and Earl Raab, *The Politics of Unreason* (New York: Harper & Row, 1970).

21. Lipset and Raab, *Ibid.*, p. 14.

22. These distinctions are suggested by Gianfranco Pasquino and Donatella della Porta, "Interpretations of Italian Left-Wing Terrorism" (a paper delivered at the XII World Congress of the International Political Science Association, Rio De Janeiro, August 9-14, 1982); and Donatella della Porta, "le cause del terrorismo nelle societa contemporanee," in Donatella della Porta and Gianfranco Pasquino (eds.), *Terrorismo e violenza politica* (Bologna: Il Mulino, 1983) pp. 19–38.

23. Sabino Acquaviva, *Il seme religioso della rivolta* (Milan: Rusconi libri, 1979) pp. 16–42; and *Guerriglia e guerra rivoluzionaria in Italia* (Milan: Rizzoli editore, 1979) pp. 17–28; see also Franco Ferrarotti, *L'ipnosi della violenza* (Milan: Rizzoli editore, 1980) pp. 36–51.

24. Franco Ferrarotti, *Fascismo di ritorno* (Rome: Edizioni delle lega per le autonomie e i poteri locali, 1973); Giovanni Verni, *Dalla resistenza ad oggi* (Rome: Edizioni della lega per le autonomie e i poteri locali, 1975); Enzo Santarelli, *Facismo e neofascismo* (Rome: Editore Riuniti, 1974).

25. della Porta and Pasquino, "Interpretations of Italian left-Wing Terrorism," *op. cit.*, pp. 19–20.

26. Alberto Ronchey, *Accade in Italia 1968–1977* (Milan: Garzanti editore, 1977) pp. 92–100.

27. Giovanna Guidorossi, *Gli italiani e la politica* (Milan: Franco Angelli editore, 1984) pp. 59–65.

28. Gianfranco Pasquino, "Difference e somiglianze per una ricerca sul terrorismo italiano," in della Porta and Pasquino (eds.), *Terrorismo e violenza politica op. cit.*, pp. 237–263.

29. Ugo Finetti, *Il Dissenso nel PCI* (Milan: Sugar edizioni, 1978) pp. 164–292.

30. Petra Rosenbaum, *Il nuovo fascismo* (Milan: Feltrinelli, 1975) pp. 206–213.

31. See for example, Corrado Strajano, *L'Italia Nichilista* (Milan: Mondadori editore, 1982); Giorgia Manzini, *Indagine su un brigatista rosso* (Turin: Einaudi, 1978); and Giampaolo Pansa, *Storie italiane di violenza e terrorismo* (Rome: Laterza, 1980).

32. Giorgio Bocca, *Il terrorismo italiano* (Milan: Rizzoli editore, 1978) pp. 7–22.

33. Mino Monicelli, *L'Ultrasinistra in Italia 1968–1978* (Bari: Laterza, 1978) pp. 33–41.

34. For different perspectives on this theme see Alberto Melucci, *L'Invenzione del presente* (Bologna: Il Mulino, 1982) pp. 161–232; and D.A. Strickland and Peter P. Krauss, "Political Disintegration and Latent Terror," in Michael Stohl (ed.), *The Politics of Terrorism*, 2nd ed. (New York: Marcell Dekker, Inc., 1983) pp. 77–117.

35. Paulo Guzzanti, *Il neofascismo e le sue organizzazioni paramiliteri* (Rome: PSI, 1973) pp. 7-31: Giampaolo Pansa, *Borghese mi ha detto* (Milan: Palazzi editore, 1971) pp. 155-185.

36. Charles Tilly, Louise Tilly and Richard Tilly;, *The Rebellious Century* (Cambridge, Mass.: Harvard University Press, 1975) pp. 304-309.

37. Alessandro Coletti, *Anarchici e questori* (Padova: Marsilio editori, 1971) pp. 7-8.

38. Quoted in George Woodcock, *Anarchism* (New York: Meridian Books, 1962) p. 337.

39. Pier Carlo Masini, *Storia degli anarchici italiani nell' epoca degli attentati* (Milan: Rizzoli editore, 1981); Roman Canosa and Amadeo Santuosso, *Magistrati, anarchici e socialisti* (Milan: Feltrinelli, 1981).

40. For accounts see Manlio Cancogni, *Gli squadristi* (Milan: Longanesi & Co., 1980); Renzo De Felice, *Mussolini il fascista: la conquista del potere 1921-1925* (Turin: Einaudi editore, 1966).

41. Sergio Pannunzio, *Diritto, forza e violenza* (Bologna: Biblioteca di studi sociali, 1921) pp. 40-45.

42. Carlo Marletti, "imagine, pubblicitte e ideologia del terrorismo," in Bonante (ed.), *Dimensioni del terrorismo politico op. cit.,* pp. 203-212.

43. For an account of the event see Denis Mack Smith, *Mussolini* (New York: Vintage Books, 1982) pp. 74-79.

44. Charles Delzell, *Mussolini's Enemies* (Princeton, N.J.: Princeton University Press, 1961) pp. 158-160.

45. Mack Smith, *op. cit.,* pp. 143-145.

46. Delzell, *op. cit.,* p. 107.

47. Giorgio Bocca, *Storia dell'Italia partigiana* (Bari: Laterza, 1977) pp. 135-141, 207-215.

48. Soccorso Rosso (eds.), *Brigate Rosse* (Milan: Feltrinelli, 1976) p. 14.

49. Pier Guiseppe Murgia, *Ritorneremo* (Milan: Sugar edizioni, 1976) p. 110.

50. Miriam Mafai, *L'Uomo che sognava la lotta armata* (Milan: Rizzoli editore, 1984) p. 71.

51. The list is drawn from Pietro Secchia, *Lotta antifascista e giovani generazioni* (Milan: La Pietra, 1973) pp. 80-103. For the atmosphere inside a neo-fascist youth group in Rome during this period, see Giulio Salierno, *Autobiografia di un picchiatore fascista* (Turin: Einaudi editore, 1976).

3
BLACK TERRORISM:
THE NEO-FASCISTS, 1969–1984

As we have sought to make clear, political terrorism in Italy did not begin in 1969. It is true, nevertheless, that the wave of mass student and worker protest that swept the country in 1968–69 created conditions which served to raise radically the level of political violence. The purpose of this chapter and the next one is to provide an account of political terrorism in Italy from 1969 through the early 1980s. Yet before beginning this commentary some general observations are necessary.

First, there are really two separate stories to be told. There is the story of terrorism initiated by neo-Fascist organizations and the story of the violence committed by the leftist revolutionary groups. The political ideas that inspired them, the organizations they formed and the deeds they committed were sufficiently dissimilar to require separate accounts if we are to understand what happened.

Second, during the recent episode of terrorist activity, Italy experienced not one but two outbreaks of mass upheaval. The first, to which reference had been made repeatedly, occurred in 1968–69. In these years, university students, reacting to developments abroad (Vietnam, the examples of their cohorts in France and the United States) as well as long-term dissatisfaction with the structure of higher education in their own country, shut down faculties and marched through the streets of the major cities of central and northern Italy. The revolt of the students became linked to the cause of Italian workers. During the 'hot autumn' of 1969, as labor contracts came up for renewal, hundreds of thousands of workers engaged in wildcat strikes, mass marches and other forms of labor agitation in an effort not only to improve their wages, hours and working conditions, but also to redefine the nature of their work situations. New forms of worker organizations were created inside plants and factories aimed at restructuring worker management relations in ways that would modify their traditionally authoritarian format.[1]

These events served to precipitate an increase in terrorist activity for the next half decade. But by the period 1975–76, the wave of political violence unleashed by the first upheaval was on the wane. The major neo-Fascist organizations of the era had been dissolved by the authorities, and many of their leaders and militants had been jailed or had fled into exile after their plans had failed. Likewise, the first wave of left-wing terrorist groups seemed on the verge of extinction. Most members of the Red Brigades' 'historic nucleus' were in prison awaiting trial. Other groups, notably the Nuclei of Armed Proletarians (NAP), had been decimated as a result of vigorous police work and their own ineptitude.

Yet just as terrorism appeared to be subsiding, there occurred another upheaval. The stagflation of the economy, brought on by rapid increases in oil prices and the declining ability of Italian goods to compete in international markets, stimulated a rise in the unemployment rate. The universities, whose admission standards had been reformed and lowered, were turning out new *laureati* for whom there were no jobs. Expectations—raised by the dramatic advances made by the Communists in the 1975 regional elections—that the Christian Democrats (DC) might be expelled from power at the national level were dashed by the outcome of the 1976 general election. These events served to re-ignite political terrorism. A second and far more destructive generation of terrorists and terrorist groups began their attacks.

The structure of these chapters reflect the above considerations. Specifically, these provide separate descriptions of neo-Fascist and revolutionary terrorism, and each of the two chapters is subdivided into accounts of the first and second generation of terrorist activities in Italy.

Neo-Fascist Ideology

By far the most deadly acts of political violence committed during the first generation of political terrorism were ones inflicted by neo-Fascist organizations. These were the *stragi* or massacres. The most destructive of these events were the bombings at the National Agricultural Bank at Piazza Fontana in Milan in December 1969 that killed 17 people, and two events in 1974: the bomb explosion during an anti-Fascist demonstration at Piazza La Loggia in Brescia that left eight dead and the derailment of the express train *Italicus* near Bologna in which another 12 individuals were murdered. As in the case of any crime, political or otherwise, the best way in which to begin analysis is by asking, why?

An inquiry into the motives of the neo-Fascists should begin with an understanding of the anti-democratic political ideas which inspired their behavior. This observation is not as obvious as it may seem. Other than a visceral anti-Communism, a perception of violence and warfare as manly pursuits and a nostalgia for Mussolini's dictatorship, some observers of Italian political life have been reluctant to see the neo-Fascists as possessed of any serious ideas about society and politics.[2] But this judgment is an erroneous one. The neo-Fascist terrorists did indeed have ideas and principles which ought to be taken seriously if for no other reason than the violent neo-Fascists themselves took them very seriously.[3]

The principal Italian writers from whose works they derived their conceptions were Julio Cesare Evola and his philosophical disciples: Adriano Romualdi and Giorgio Freda. The three are bound together by, among other things, the fact that during the 1950s they were members of the Italian Social Movement (MSI). Evola was a minor figure during the Fascist era who spent most of World War II living in Munich and working for the Nazi SS. His early writings had little impact on Mussolini or other Fascist ideologues. In any number of ways he was critical of Mussolini and his regime.[4]

A complete explication of Evola's ideas and those of his followers is beyond the scope of this study (one partial bibliography of Evola's writings is more than three pages in length).[5] Instead, let us focus on certain of their core ideas.

To begin, these writers share a "spiritual" and organic conception of man, one radically different, as they conceive it, from the materialistic, individualist and collectivist premises of capitalists, liberals, Marxists and Zionists now dominant in the western world.[6] Man only achieves his full potential when he abandons his concern for material comfort and pursues a life animated by heroism and adventure. Human beings are inherently unequal; some, an aristocracy of the spirit, exhibit nobler and more adventurous spirits than others. A leadership caste composed of warriors is the ideal.[7]

Central to Evola's thought is the celebration of the traditional and the denigration of the modern. The products of the French Revolution—liberalism, mass democracy, socialism, radicalism and finally Communism—are manifestations of the decadence and perversion of the modern spirit. Modern western societies which exemplify these doctrines are held up against the traditional ones of Sparta, Rome and Prussia. These societies exhibited the values Evola identified with the traditional; they were organic, hierarchic and virile.

Can such values by recaptured in the modern era? Evola, hardly an optimist, thought they might. He and his followers saw some positive signs in seemingly disparate groups and cultures. The "heroism" and self-sacrifice in a lost cause of the Waffen SS was idealized. The Islamic concept of Jihad and the Japanese code of Bushido were seen as expressions of the traditional spirit. Surprisingly, kind things were written about the forces unleashed by China's Great Cultural Revolution. Also surprisingly, the historic fascism held in esteem was not that of Mussolini, too much populistic demagoguery, but that of its more spiritual variants: the Rumanian Iron Guard and the Spanish Falange.

On the theme of the relationship between state and society, Evola, Romualdi and Freda exalt the former over the latter. The spirit of the ideal state is masculine and commanding or pedagogic. Society is defined as feminine, passive and susceptible to chaos and disintegration without a vigorous state to control it.

But is such a state possible in the modern world, and if so what form would it take? The two obvious models, American and Soviet, are held up to ridicule. Like the United States, the states of the European Community are pervaded by the spirit of "Judeo-capitalism" (Anti-Semitism is a recurring theme for Evola and his followers) and controlled by the corrupt and materialistic bourgeoisie. In short, none of the extant systems of government provide plausible alternatives for Italy's degenerate regime.

The views of Romualdi and Freda, though both derivative from Evola's, diverge on this matter. For Romualdi, there already existed elements within the Italian state in which to place some hope. Bearing in mind that Evola saw in the warrior and in orders of warriors, the highest ideals of human attainment, Romualdi looked to the 'separate corps' of the Italian state for salvation. The military and the police should be encouraged to assume national leadership because only they had the capacity to become Evola's warriors.

Yet left to themselves the 'separate corps' were not likely to achieve an awareness of what was necessary. They needed the encouragement and support that could be furnished by political forces. These forces were not those of a parliamentary political party but that of a national movement capable of generating enthusiasm among patriotic Italians. Anti-Communism, a reaction to the subversive designs of the Communists on Italian society, could create the bonds necessary to put this alliance into place and install its elite in power.

By descending from Evola's metaphysical pronouncements to the all too mundane world of Italian politics, Romualdi produced an argument in favor of a coup d'état and military dictatorship. His views were to prove influential among leaders of the first generation of neo-Fascist groups that used terrorism in an attempt to achieve a conservative revolution. If not a precise blueprint for action, Romualdi provided leaders of the New Order, National Vanguard and the National Front with a general sense of direction.

The theoretical justifications for the behavior of the second wave of neo-Fascist organizations, those that were active in the second half of the 1970s, were provided by the writings of Giorgio Freda. While Romualdi was calling for a revolution from above, Freda's work offered a rationale for a popular insurrection. As a disciple of Evola, Freda desired a society in which egoistic and materialist values would be transcended by spiritual ones, but the means for attaining such a transcendence were not ones which the 'separate corps' would approve.

Freda defined his country's situation as one in which there existed a state dominated by and committed to the defense of the bourgeoisie. It is beyond reorganization or redemption even by its warriors. The objective must be to subvert it. To this end, it may even be necessary to forge a common outlook with all those elements in Italian society which are intent on the same goal, even left-wing youth. The existing order must be replaced by a "popular state". The latter would eliminate most forms of private property and replace existing forms of political representation with functional representation. At the apex of the new regime, there will be a presidium of state, a committee which in turn will select a regent. The latter would be responsible for the coordination of all state activities. A curious blend of Evola's ideas with some derived from Marx—some observers would refer to it as "Nazi-Maoism"—Freda's concoction could achieve some impact on the Nuclei of Armed Revolutionaries and Third Position.[8]

The First Generation

Most of the forces that would take part in the escalation of neo-Fascist violence were in place well before the 'hot autumn' of 1969. The first such group to be organized was the New Order. Begun as a faction within the MSI in the early 1950s, it was led by young veterans of the armed forces of Mussolini's Social Republic, notably Giuseppe "Pino" Rauti and Clemente Graziani. The New Order represented the element within the MSI that was most taken by Evola's work. As against an MSI leadership that in these years was committed to the pursuit of alliances with monarchists, liberals and conservative Christian Democrats, this "spiritualist" faction propounded an alternative strategy for neo-Fascist advances. One observer quotes Rauti as saying the following at an MSI meeting in Rome in 1952: "I don't believe in elections, I don't believe in parties, and I don't believe that Parliament represents the nation. I am convinced, therefore, that we must change tactics and strategy if we want to count for something in our country. We must be wolves and make ourselves known as such."[9] Rauti then went on to outline a series of measures, including physical attacks on leftist organizations and the formation of closer ties with the armed forces, that would result in a rightist revival in Italy.

At the MSI's tumultuous 1956 national congress at Milan, the Movement's secretary, Arturo Michelini, proposed a resolution which called for the achievement of a formal alliance with Italy's conservative parties, a rec-

TABLE 3.1
Percentage of Italian Students Voting for the Neo-Fascist Slate at
University Elections

Academic Year	Per Cent Vote for Neo-Fascist Slate*
1951–52	17.24
1952–53	15.78
1953–54	14.88
1955–56	13.22
1956–57	16.32
1957–58	14.64
1958–59	13.86
1959–60	13.83
1961–62	14.57
1962–63	14.39
1963–64	11.65
1964–65	14.17

*The neo-Fascist student group affiliated with the MSI was the
Fronte universitario di azione nazionale (FAUN).

Source: Guiliano Urbani, Politica e Universitari (Florence: Sansoni
editore, 1966) p. 76.

ommendation justified in terms of anti-Communist solidarity (this was in
the aftermath of the Soviet intervention in Hungary). The approval of the
resolution, by a narrow margin, produced the withdrawal of the spiritualists
from the MSI. Rauti, Graziani, Paolo Signrelli, Stefano Delle Chiaie and
other future leaders of the neo-Fascist terrorism departed in order to form
a separate organization, the New Order (ON).

Over the next decade ON was able to recruit a membership numbering
in the thousands, including Giorgio Freda, with particular strength in the
Veneto, Campania and Sicily. From where did such support come?

No precise answer to this question is possible. Nonetheless, it at least
seems worthwhile to make the following observation. In recent years most
commentaries about Italian terrorism have emphasized the attraction the
left-wing revolutionary groups have had among university students. The
accuracy of this appraisal seems indisputable. Yet it should not be forgotten
that in the 1950s and early 1960s, neo-Fascism also was not without substantial
support among Italian students. Election results (see Table 3.1) for student
government representatives at universities throughout the country from the
early 1950s to the mid-1960s suggest a substantial proportion of students
were willing to vote for candidates of a youth organization affiliated with

the MSI. In fact, during this period, the level of support enjoyed by neo-Fascist candidates at the student elections was about twice that of MSI candidates at national elections for the Chamber of Deputies.

If we combine the popularity of neo-Fascism among students with the fact that during the same period the MSI leadership was committed to a policy of legitimizing itself by pursuing coalitions with the conservative parties, it is not hard to speculate about the composition of the New Order. The hypothesis that suggests itself is that numbers of MSI students alienated by the Movement's conservative direction found their way into the New Order and other radical neo-Fascist groupings. The biographies, to be discussed more fully in the next chapter, of some of the prominent figures involved in the New Order and other groups exhibit a pattern of youthful participation in the MSI followed by disenchantment, withdrawal and affiliation with one of the more militant neo-Fascist organizations, a form of youth rebellion well before the explosion of 1968 took many university students in a very different political direction.

> We are an elite of heroes. Heroic in fact is our style of life, rich in values that alone permits us to approach the divine, heroic is our battle against a system that violates and oppresses us, heroic is our commitment to the forces of honor, loyalty and discipline.[10]

The sentiment is pure Evola, but the rhetoric is that of Stefano Delle Chiaie, the founder and leader of National Vanguard. Later to be nicknamed the "Black Bombardier" because of his terrorist activities in Rome during the late 60s and early 70s, Delle Chiaie's political career parallels that of his friend "Pino" Rauti. But Delle Chiaie broke with the New Order in 1960 and created his own neo-Fascist organization. In addition to his commitment to Evola's philosophy, Delle Chiaie was an ardent believer in a conspiracy theory, according to which the Communists were behind all events he judged harmful to the Italian nation. His hope was that at moments of maximum peril, the 'sane' forces in the country would step forward and rescue it from the Communist menace. In this instance, he sought to fulfill his own hope.

Even before the 1968–69 crisis produced a renewal of his organization, the National Vanguard engaged in a variety of acts of 'neo-squadrism'. Rome, and especially its university, was the locale for many of these punitive expeditions. Illustratively, a student, Paolo Rossi, was killed during a scuffle between a National Vanguard contingent and a leftist student group in 1966. In addition to Rome, Delle Chiaie's organization was able to put down roots in several southern regions, including Campania, Puglia and Sicily, as well as in some of the major northern cities, Milan and Turin in particular. At the height of its activities, its membership was estimated to be 2,000.[11] These adherents were organized, in classic Fascist manner, into action squads, small units whose members stood ready to intervene against leftist manifestations.

The New Order and National Vanguard along with two smaller groups, the Revolutionary Action Movement (MAR) of Carlo Fumagalli, an ex-partisan, and the Integralist Movement led by Sandro Saccucci, a former military officer, were the early groups to emerge among the first generation of violent neo-Fascist organizations; others would be formed as the turbulence mounted in the late 60s. Before describing their formation, it is necessary to note some crucial political developments.

In 1964 the Center-Left coalition government of Christian Democrats and Socialists entered into crisis. The Socialist party under the leadership of Pietro Nenni became reluctant to continue its alliance with the Christian Democrats for reasons having to do with the latter's refusal to implement the Center-Left's legislative program. When the Socialists withdrew their support in the summer of 1964, the country was without a government. In this context, one which included the fact that many conservative leaders had been hostile to Socialist participation in the government from the start, Antonio Segni, the President of Italy, held a meeting with General Giovanni De Lorenzo, head of the *Carabinieri*. Later to be the subject of a formal parliamentary inquiry, journalists' reports of this discussion had Segni telling the general to hold his forces in and around Rome ready for all eventualities.[12] Segni later denied having instructed De Lorenzo to prepare for a possible military intervention. Nonetheless, later investigations disclosed a number of troubling facts. For one, Nenni related that it was out of concern with the danger of military intervention that he quickly agreed to have his party resume its support for the government. For another, several years before his meeting with Segni, De Lorenzo, then head of Italy's military intelligence service, had proposed plan "Solo", a scheme with just such an end in mind. Other disclosures about the intelligence service (SIFAR) included the fact that it had kept dossiers on many of the country's political leaders, leftist ones in particular, and had provided covert funding for a number of patriotic organizations, including veterans groups and, most disturbing, the New Order and National Vanguard. The scandal that followed these revelations led to the reorganization of the intelligence service in 1967. Yet, as we shall see, the reform did not silence continuing claims of "occult" links between the intelligence service and the neo-Fascist groups.

In the spring of 1965, less than a year after the Segni–De Lorenzo encounter, another meeting occurred in Rome. This event, a series of seminars, was sponsored by a previously unknown Institute for Historical and Military Studies and held in a deluxe hotel. The subjects discussed were revolutionary warfare and counter-insurgency. Participants included leading military and intelligence officers along with luminaries from other areas of government and private business. The backgrounds of several participants included involvement in Mussolini's Social Republic. Among the speakers were the SIFAR officers Guido Giannettini, later to be tried in connection with the Piazza Fontana massacre, and "Pino" Rauti, whose talk was devoted to an analysis of Communist penetration in Italy.[13] Among the "students" in attendance were Mario Merlino and Stefano Delle Chiaie from the National Vanguard.

The preoccupation with revolutionary warfare and counterinsurgency is not hard to understand. The French experiences in Indochina and Algeria and the growing American involvement in Vietnam were not far below the surface. As part of their worldwide plan of conquest, the Communists were viewed as fully capable of launching their schemes in Italy, indeed Communist attempts to transform the Resistance into a social revolution were cited. The issue was how to prevent the plan of conquest from achieving its objectives in Italy.

It is not necessary to claim that this meeting in Rome was the place where a conspiracy was devised. It is sufficient to call attention to the mentality expressed at the meeting, specifically a mentality, not unknown in the United States, that saw the Communists under whatever guise they presented themselves as embarked on a design to conquer power in Italy by any means at their disposal. The Communist conspiracy had been uncovered. The need for counterinsurgency or counter-mobilization was manifest. Further, in this context it is not hard to imagine the impact the student and worker protests of 1968–69 were to have on this mentality. Reality began to confirm the fear.

Under the heading of counter-mobilization, various events occurred between the Rome meeting and the 'hot autumn' of 1969 that need to be mentioned. At the international level, there was a military coup against the democratic regime in Greece in 1967, brought on in part by violent left-wing protests. In 1968 a delegation of Italian neo-Fascists visited Greece to confer with spokesmen of the new military rulers. In addition, the impact of the Vietnam War was beginning to reach Italy. Protests against American participation in the war were occurring with increasing frequency. Some of the demonstrations were organized by the Communist party. Reactions to Vietnam in the United States captured the imaginations of many Italians, particularly university students.

It was during this period that new neo-Fascist groups were formed. The National Front headed by Prince Valerio Borghese was organized in 1968. A glamorous military figure, Borghese had been a submarine commander in the early stages of World War II and later became leader of an anti-partisan unit during the Social Republic period.[14] For the latter involvement, he was tried and convicted of war crimes in 1949. After his release, he became active in the MSI. But in the early 1960s, Borghese's interest in the tepid brand of right-wing politics the MSI practiced under Michelini waned, and he drifted away. The prince was a man who professed commitments to Italian nationalism, the maintenance of order and the restoration of public authority.[15] To express these values he organized first a patriotic society, the Tricolor Committee, and later, the National Front. Unlike the New Order or the National Vanguard, with their appeal to neo-Fascist students and other young people, Borghese could rally to his organization middle-aged veterans of the Social Republic, businessmen and military officers who had never reconciled themselves to parliamentary democracy. And if the resurgent neo-Fascists were to have a new Mussolini, Borghese, at the age of 62, was it.

As an organization, the National Front was divided into "delegations" of recruits organized in various cities. In turn, the delegations were subdivided in two parts: visible groups of frontists for encounters with the public and armed subterranean units prepared to strike when the appropriate time came. In this connection, the Front could also count on the support of the New Order and National Vanguard.

Also in these years, a much smaller group was formed in the Veneto region of northeast Italy. Led by Giorgio Freda and Giovanni Ventura, this formation, with ties to the New Order, went through a series of name changes—Young Europe, Aryan Aristocracy, Group for The Defense of the State.[16] Freda and Ventura had similar backgrounds; both came from pro-Fascist families, both had joined the MSI as young students and both had left it because of its abandonment, as they saw it, of authentic Fascist values. These are familiar stories by now.

In the three years preceding the Piazza Fontana bank bombing, an act for which they would be prosecuted, Freda and Ventura engaged in a variety of literary pursuits. In 1966 they sent letters to 2,000 army officers which encouraged their readers to rebel and seize power. They published a periodical, *Reaction*, whose title aptly characterized its contents. And in 1968 they opened bookstores in Padua and Treviso. Publicly professing conversions to Marxism-Leninism, their stores were filled with the writings of Lenin, Mao, Rosa Luxumburg and other revolutionary theoreticians. In other words, they sought to create new identities for themselves as left-wing figures.

The attempt by neo-Fascists to establish new political identities on the Left was not restricted to Freda and Ventura. In Rome, Mario Merlino and other members of Delle Chiaie's National Vanguard formed the 22nd of March group. Taking its name from the date of the student uprising at the University of Nanterre in France, an event that had occurred two months before its establishment, this group professed a commitment to anarchism.[17] The meaning of this behavior seems clear. Freda and Ventura's "conversion" to Marxism-Leninism and the formation of March 22 were intended to provide a cover by which the neo-Fascists could commit acts of violence and disruption disguised to make them appear as if young leftists were responsible. The context was 1968, the year of the student rebellion.

The speed of the neo-Fascist counter-mobilization increased over the course of 1968. As disclosed by subsequent judicial investigations, the Freda-Ventura group in the Veneto and the National Vanguard in Rome committed a series of anonymous bombings. Later Delle Chiaie would be prosecuted in *absentia*, on the basis of testimony provided by a former member of National Vanguard, for detonating a bomb in front of an elementary school.[18]

In addition to these covert and obviously provocative activities, 1968 also witnessed numerous exhibitions of quite open neo-Fascist violence. Most commonly, these took the form of attacks by neo-Fascist squads from New Order, National Vanguard and MSI youth groups against the left-wing student protesters at the major university centers.

Disturbing as these events were, they could not compare with what happened in 1969 and the ensuing years. In the midst of continuing student upheaval and the formation of militant New Left movements which it spawned, the workers began their struggles. Losing confidence in the ability of the dominant political parties to press their concerns on government, the three major labor federations reached agreement on a policy of circumventing the parties and articulating their proposals directly.[19] Many young workers expressed their dissatisfactions through the new revolutionary movements.

The neo-Fascists rose to the occasion. New groups were organized all over the country. Mussolini Action Squads took to the streets in Milan and engaged in battles with the new leftists. Para-military training camps were set-up in the Appenines, in the Dolomites, in Umbria and on the slopes of Mount Etna in Sicily. The MSI went through a process of renewal. Michelini, the Movement's long-time secretary, died and his place was taken by Giorgio Almirante, leader of its less inhibited faction. "Pino" Rauti was sufficiently impressed by the change of direction that he rejoined the MSI, taking some of his New Order followers along with him. As may be imagined, the MSI's new leadership did little to restrain the Movement's youth groups from their, by this point, almost daily acts of street violence.[20]

It is true that the bombing of the National Agricultural Bank at Piazza Fontana on December 12, 1969 was the first successful massacre. However, there were other attempts that preceded it. Aside from Delle Chiaie's exploits in Rome almost a year earlier, bombs had been planted on several trains during the summer of 1969. And at almost the same time as the fatal Piazza Fontana explosion, other bombs were set-off in public places in Rome. Fortunately, no one was killed as the result of these attempts.

As the neo-Fascists had hoped—and their hopes apparently rested on more than guesswork—the police in Milan responded quickly to the massacre. Two anarchists, Giuseppe Pinelli and Pietro Valpreda, were arrested and accused of the crime. The expectation was that outraged Italians who had witnessed the student and worker disturbances would draw the appropriate conclusions. But this was not to be. Within several days of the arrests, one of the anarchists, Pinelli, died as the result of a fall from a window at the Milanese police headquarters. The police account claimed suicide, but the story was greeted with skepticism.

By February 1970, news stories appeared about Piazza Fontana which pointed in another direction.[21] A young school teacher from Treviso had gone to an investigating magistrate and testified that a friend of his, Giovanni Ventura, had told him that he and Freda, along with other neo-Fascists, were responsible for Piazza Fontana and other bombings.[22] The investigation yielded indictments against the neo-Fascists which, in turn, led to an extraordinarily complex legal process, the site of their trial being moved from Milan to Rome to Catanzaro. Along the way, the obviously innocent Valpreda was kept in prison for years, one of the policemen involved in the original investigation was murdered, and several military intelligence officers were indicted. Freda and Ventura escaped confinement only to be found in South America and extradited back to Italy. These adventures were to culminate, more than a decade after the bombing, when the Court of Cassation, Italy's highest appeals court, overturned the trial court's decision by annulling the convictions.[23]

After Piazza Fontana, the next major attempt by neo-Fascists to exploit the wave of political turmoil began in the summer of 1970 at the other end of the Italian peninsula. After years of prolonged debate, the country's Center-Left government finally enacted a law providing for the formation of regional governments. In this context the national government decided to make Catanzaro, rather then Reggio Calabria, the site of Calabria's new regional government. This decision outraged citizens of the latter city. If Reggio Calabria had been selected, the community would have received public service jobs and other benefits that went with the designation as regional capital. Because of the city's high unemployment rate, the loss was felt to be considerable. In July 1970, a city-wide general strike was proclaimed. Mass disturbances and attacks on various public buildings followed.

In these circumstances, Borghese, along with other members of the National Front, as well as sympathetic contingents from the New Order, National Vanguard and MSI, arrived in the city.[24] Despite the neo-Fascists' long held opposition to all forms of regional decentralization, they proceeded to hold a series of conferences denouncing the government's action and proclaiming their fidelity to the cause of the exploited South. And notwithstanding a visit to Reggio Calabria by ministers from Rome, accompanied by offers of compromise and conciliation, the mass protests continued for months.

The situation in the northern and central parts of the country were not tranquil either. Not only were there recurrent clashes between leftist students and neo-Fascist squads in and around the universities throughout 1970, but there was an abundance of neo-Fascist terrorism as well. To cite two examples: in May several members of a neo-Fascist group were arrested for attempting to dynamite a passenger train bound from Genoa to Rome; on another occasion, members of the Revolutionary Action Movement (MAR) were caught while attempting to blow up power lines near the city of Sondrio in Lombardy.[25]

Finally, during the evening of December 7-8, 1970, there is evidence that a coup d'état was attempted. On that occasion, groups of neo-Fascists, including squads from New Order, National Vanguard and the National Front, gathered around major government buildings in Rome, including the interior ministry and the headquarters of the state run radio-television network. The squadrists waited for a signal from Borghese, one which never came. Dispirited (there was a torrential rain that night), they dispersed.

The facts in this case are not completely public, but, based on subsequent judicial and parliamentary investigations, this much seems clear. The episode did in fact occur; it was not the product of the imaginations of Roman journalists. Borghese, who later died in exile, and other neo-Fascist leaders were tried and convicted of the attempt. Further, the effort would not have been contemplated without its tacit endorsement by individuals who wielded more power than that possessed by the several hundred squadrists gathered on Roman street corners. Accordingly, in October 1974, several police and military officers, including the former commander of the Italian air force, were arrested and accused of complicity in the affair. The degree of personal and financial involvement of members of the intelligence service (SID) and the Masonic lodge *Propaganda Due* still seems obscure.[26]

Over the next several years, the neo-Fascists tended to repeat the pattern established in 1969-70.[27] In cities like Milan, Rome, and Naples there were regular street battles with leftist groups, or attacks on isolated individuals if the opportunity arose. This type of squadrism was coupled with efforts to plant explosives on trains or railroad tracks and at other locations where they were likely to do as much damage as possible.

It was in this context that the 1972 parliamentary elections occurred. Under Almirante's leadership, the MSI proclaimed the need for a restoration of law and order in the country and appealed for the support of a silent majority of Italians tired of the upheaval. MSI spokesmen asserted the need for a restoration of authority and patriotism. The armed forces, they said, needed strengthening. They also expressed admiration for the Gaullist regime in France. On the question of violence, Almirante said that it was exclusively the work of "reds."[28] With these themes and with a number of retired military officers as parliamentary candidates, including General De Lorenzo from SIFAR and Admiral Gino Birindelli (a former NATO commander in the Mediterranean), the MSI came close to doubling the vote it had received in the 1968 balloting.

Yet neither the electoral success of the MSI, nor the continued exhibition of violence by the New Order, National Vanguard and the other neo-Fascist formations produced any dramatic results, at least not ones desired by the Right. Worse still, in 1973 the police succeeded in uncovering another organization committed to toppling the democratic regime, one engaged in preparations to achieve this end. This was the *Rosa dei Venti*, a federation of neo-Fascist groups operating throughout the country. The leaders of the *Rosa dei Venti* were ideologically committed to the principles of Mussolini's Social Republic. Indeed, some of those arrested in connection with this scheme had been members or supporters of that regime. Those for whom warrants were issued included an interesting collection of people: there were lawyers, physicians and army officers up to the rank of general. Further, the project had also received the financial support of a number of wealthy industrialists.[29] Again, as in the case of Borghese's National Front, the question of the existence of "occult" forces behind the *Rosa dei Venti*, specifically the Masonic lodge *Propaganda Due*, continues to be a matter of investigation.

Nineteen seventy-four was the last year in which the strategy of tensions, as this pattern of neo-Fascist action came to be called, was seriously pursued. Among other things, it was the year in which a national referendum was held on a law concerning civil divorce. The bitter campaign launched in connection with the referendum, one in which the Christian Democrats and MSI campaigned against, and the other major parties for, the law, served to exacerbate the already high level of tension in the country. Accordingly, there were two massacres during the year. The first occurred in Brescia at the end of May. A bomb was set-off in the middle of a peaceful outdoor rally called to protest the persistence of widespread neo-Fascist squadrism in the community. Eight people were killed and 94 injured.[30] The second slaughter occurred in August when the express train *Italicus* was derailed by a dynamite charge as it emerged from a tunnel near Bologna. The toll in this instance was 12 dead and 105 injured. The responsibility for both events was that of the neo-Fascists, large numbers of whom were arrested because of their involvement. But the final results of the prosecutions undertaken against the accused neo-Fascists were much like those achieved in the Piazza Fontana case. Two convictions were obtained in the Brescia case, but both were later overturned by an appeal court's ruling. The latter decision came too late to do one of the neo-Fascist criminals any good. Ermano Buzzi was strangled to death in prison by two other neo-Fascists imprisoned for their involvements in other political murders. Rumor had it that Buzzi had been prepared to tell the court what he knew about other neo-Fascists involved in the Brescia massacre.[31]

The prosecution against those New Order adherents accused of the *Italicus* murders lasted longer but resulted in the dismissal of the charges against the accused because of insufficient evidence. Nonetheless, the trial court did take note of the possibility that *Propaganda Due*, as well as members of SID, could be implicated in the massacre.[32]

Nineteen seventy-four ended with yet another attempt at mass murder. Mario Tuti, the leader of a small band of self-defined revolutionary Fascists, placed a bomb on the railroad tracks near Arezzo in Tuscany. The bomb was detected before it could be detonated, and Tuti, along with his followers, was caught later by the police, though two officers were killed in the process. Unlike the Brescia and *Italicus* cases, Tuti and the members of his band were convicted for this crime, and their convictions were upheld by the appeals court.[33]

The government in Rome and many state prosecutors around the country were not oblivious to the neo-Fascists' threat to Italian democracy.

Nineteen seventy-four was also the year in which they chose to react massively to the threat. Mariano Rumor, the Christian Democratic prime minister, and his government decided to form a special organization, the General Inspectorate against Terrorism, to combat the political violence. In his announcement of the government's initiative, Rumor emphasized its particular concern with the neo-Fascists.[34] Also, proposals were introduced in Parliament to outlaw the MSI. Some neo-Fascist para-military camps were raided, and those people receiving training were arrested or, in some instances, shot by the police when they resisted.[35] In the cities, large numbers of neo-Fascists were arrested for having committed an enormous list of violent acts.

In addition to these activities, legal proceedings were undertaken against the New Order and later against the National Vanguard. Under a consti-tutional provision and a statute law enacted in 1952 to implement it, it is illegal to reconstruct the Fascist party or even advocate its reconstruction. The law has been applied selectively and sporadically over the years, but investigators and magistrates no longer ignored the Fascist character of these two organizations.[36] Thus, a Roman court found the New Order guilty under the law and imposed penal sanctions against its leaders. Following this decision, the interior minister signed a decree dissolving the organization. The immediate effect of this action was the flight of the New Order leadership (Clemente Graziani, Elio Massagrande and others) into exile in Franco's Spain. Those ON members still in Italy changed the group's name to Black Order and continued its operation on a clandestine basis.

The authorities officially dissolved the National Vanguard in 1975. Yet despite this action, Delle Chiaie, who had been sought by the police since

1970, was not caught. In exile part of this time, he continued to slip in and out of Italy to conduct his business.

By the middle of the 1970s the neo-Fascist project to promote a coup d'état had failed. The state had not collapsed despite the strategy of tensions. The two principal neo-Fascist organizations had been declared criminal associations; the National Front and the *Rosa dei Venti* had also been disbanded. Many of the key figures in neo-Fascist terrorism were in prison or exile. Further, some of their covert collaborators in the military and police establishments were beginning to be apprehended. Illustratively, Vito Miceli, former head of SID, was arrested in 1975 for his part in the neo-Fascist schemes. Those "separate corps" and "sane" forces within the state on whom the neo-Fascists had counted for help were no longer in a position to provide it.

The Second Generation Groups

It is at this point that the neo-Fascist leadership held a series of clandestine conferences which led it to a change of tactics. The meetings were held during 1975 in Albano, Corsica and Nice. Participants included Delle Chiaie, Graziani, Massagrande and Signorelli: New Order and National Vanguard leaders. These veterans of the neo-Fascist movement decided to amalgamate their organizations to carry out additional operations inside Italy. They also concluded that a coup d'état was no longer a realistic possibility. Instead, they reached agreement on the need to "disarticulate" the Italian state, the object of their now unrequited love. This judgment was one, as we shall see, which the Red Brigades (BR) had made at about the same time. In fact there was an intent to emulate the BR and other leftist groups.[37] Translated into operational terms, this meant that the neo-Fascists would now employ the tactics of their leftist counterparts and presumptive enemies by engaging in acts of self-financing (i.e., bank robberies) and self-arming (i.e., stealing guns from sporting goods stores and other weapons depositories). It also meant that magistrates and other public officials who sought to investigate neo-Fascist activities would become subject to violent retribution.

This design was put into practice quickly and almost as quickly produced another defeat. During the summer of 1976, neo-Fascists carried out a series of spectacular thefts of money and weapons in and around Rome. In addition, after several months of planning, a group led by Pier Luigi Concutelli, a former MSI activist, murdered the magistrate who had declared the New Order a Fascist organization.[38] As a result of the killing and related crimes, Concutelli and his band of New Order–National Vanguard followers were arrested, tried and convicted.[39]

With the collapse of this initiative, a largely new generation of neo-Fascist leaders and organizations emerged to take the place of the old ones.

The new wave groups were formed in Rome beginning in 1977. They represented three separate, though not completely independent, efforts: *Costruiamo l'Azione* (Let's Take Action), the Armed Revolutionary Nuclei (NAR) and Third Position (TP). Some commentary is required in order to understand the broader political situation in which these organizations conducted their activities.

Not only in Rome, but in Padua, Bologna and other cities as well, 1977 also witnessed changes in the style of leftist violence. The practice of 'diffuse' terrorism became widespread. This form of violence, associated with the Workers' Autonomous Collectives, emphasized spontaneity and represented an alternative to the clandestine and highly planned 'campaigns' launched by the Red Brigades and other groups. This 'diffuse' format appealed to and was copied by the new wave neo-Fascists. Also, the latter's own theoretical perspective underwent some interesting modifications. Still interested in Evola and in the possibility of retrieving the traditional community, young neo-Fascists became enthralled by the works of the English fantasy writer J.R.R. Tolkien. His writing (the *Hobbit* was published in Italian in 1973), with its stories of heroism and villainy in imaginary kingdoms, was understood by those neo-Fascists who attended Camp Hobbit in the summer of 1977 as portraying the kind of spiritual values in which they found great meaning.[40]

This "Tolkien Mania" may strike readers influenced by psychoanalytic concepts as a withdrawal symptom, a flight from reality. For the neo-Fascists, however, the allure of Tolkien was part of an effort to produce a new cultural outlook, one likely to attract a broad spectrum of Italian youth to their movement. The new emphasis was on the rejection of all rigid ideological understandings of politics and the distinction between left and right in particular. Accordingly, kind things were said about all movements intent on fighting imperialism, from the Argentine Montoneros to the Arab Fedayeen, and materialism, as manifested by the multinational corporations and the Italian bourgeois state. To the leftist youth the overture was, "one enemy, one struggle." This message was a far cry from the ardent anti-Communism that inspired the earlier generation of neo-Fascist terrorists. It was also an admission of error. The earlier generation had identified the youth culture of 1968 as the enemy. This generation sought to join it.

The life-span of *Costruiamo L'Azione* was not long, 1977–79. Composed of an "archipelago" of independent groups around Rome such as the Circle Drieu La Rochelle, as well as a small cluster of Northern adherents, the organization made contact with some of the left-wing terrorist groups operating in the capital, but to no avail.[41] During its brief period of terrorist activity, the organization's various components waged a campaign of 'armed propaganda' centered in Rome and including hit and run attacks on the foreign ministry, city hall and other public buildings. These operations were brought to an end in the summer and fall of 1979 when the police arrested most of those involved.

The other two neo-Fascist initiatives emerged in 1979 as *Costruiamo L'Azione* collapsed. The Nuclei of Armed Revolutionaries (NAR) was formed by dissident members of the MSI's university student organization, FUAN, in Rome. NAR was led by the brothers Valerio and Cristiano Fioravanti; Francesca Mambro, the daughter of a policeman; and Dario Pedretti, the group's theorist. NAR's terrorist operations largely recapitulated those of *Costruiamo l'Azione*. Its most widely publicized exploit was an attack on a leftist radio station in Rome, a combination of vandalism and arson.

Third Position (TP) was a more elaborate endeavor than NAR. Its leaders were the New Order veterans Paolo Signorelli, a Roman high school teacher, and Giorgio Freda, who provided philosophical guidance by correspondence from his prison cell. Organizationally Third Position represented something more than a politically motivated youth gang. Composed of several hundred activists, it was able to articulate both an open public organization, as well as a clandestine group. Furthermore, its leaders managed to establish an organizational presence not only in Rome, but also "territorial nuclei" in the Veneto, Emilia Romagna, the Marches, Lombardy, Liguria, Basilcata and Sicily.[42]

TP members, like their counterparts in NAR, carried out a large number of terrorist attacks directed against governmental targets and commercial enterprises during 1979–80. Despite these exploits, disagreements developed within both groups. How much emphasis should be placed on spontaneity versus planning? How much hierarchical control should be vested in the national leadership? Did TP have national revolutionary objectives, or was it simply the expression of the legionnaire spirit with no long-term goals? Polemics did not settle these questions.[43]

The Roman magistrate Mario Amato was given the responsibility of investigating the Rome-based activities of these neo-Fascist groups. As a result of his work, he was murdered in June 1980 by a group of assassins from NAR led by Valerio Fioravanti and Gilberto Cavallini. Five weeks later, on August 2, a bomb was detonated in the waiting room of the Bologna railroad station; the explosion coincided with the sixth anniversary of the *Italicus* massacre. The new blast was more devastating than the one it was apparently intended to commemorate. Eighty-five people were killed and more than 200 injured. It was the worst single terrorist attack in the history of republican Italy.

In reaction to these events, the authorities began a series of arrests directed against members of the new neo-Fascist groups. Fioravanti, Cavallini, Mambro and many others were captured over the next two years. Some of the terrorists were found as far away as London, but most were arrested closer to home.[44]

Because of the disclosures of several repentant members of the band, the authorities were able to prosecute successfully those responsible for the Amato slaying. In April 1984 the court sentenced Fioravanti, Cavallini, Mambro and Signorelli to life in prison, the most severe penalty under Italian law.[45]

The investigation of the railroad station massacre was a more complex undertaking. Arrested initially was Claudio Mutti (NAR), a young school teacher from Parma who was the founder of the Italian-Libyan Friendship Society. Also taken in the roundup were a Frenchman, Paul Durand, a former Paris police officer and head of the French neo-Fascist group FANE (the European National Action Federation), Luca de Crazi, a 17 year old from Bologna who reportedly had a fondness for military uniforms and a fascination with the Nazi SS, and Marco Affatigato (NAR), a friend of Mario Tuti, who was employed as a waiter in Nice, France at the time he was arrested.[46]

These arrests, and the many more that followed, had the effect of decimating both NAR and TP. They did not, however, produce quick results in the case. Some of the suspects proved to have alibis for the day of the explosion. And, as of 1984, the judicial proceeding was still in its investigatory phase. The slowness of the investigation was especially frustrating for the families of the victims, so much so that they organized an association to press for speedier results. The association circulated petitions and sponsored public rallies in an effort to pressure the government to resolve the case. The likelihood of cooperation between the Italian neo-Fascists and similar formations in West Germany and France has made the investigation an exceedingly complicated one. And the record concerning the other major neo-Fascist massacres did not leave observers with grounds for much optimism in this case.

Summary

Neo-Fascist violence during the current era of Italian terrorism clearly underwent a process of evolution. The first wave was characterized by an effort to promote military intervention and a coup d'état. The forms of violence, a combination of street confrontations with leftists and anonymous bombings, were clearly intended to achieve this objective. Also, the evidence seems sufficient to conclude that there were elements within the police and military establishments who, fearful of Communist advances, were willing to provide the neo-Fascists with assistance. It seems likely that some members of the Masonic Lodge *Propaganda Due*, which included police and military officers, took park in these anti-democratic schemes.

The actions taken by the neo-Fascist leaders in reaction to the student protests, displays of worker militancy and Communist electoral gains, should be seen as rational and instrumental measures, that is, given the way they saw the world. But if this is so, what should we make of the second wave of neo-Fascist violence?

Costruiamo l'Azione, NAR and TP were groups whose leaders could not have held out any reasonable expectations that their behavior would lead to the violent overthrow of the democratic regime. Nor could the prospect of an alliance with the leftist revolutionaries, to whom Fascism was anathema, seem particularly plausible. From the tone of their rhetoric and the nature of their action, we are drawn to the conclusion that the second wave of neo-Fascist terrorists were motivated more by expressive than instrumental purposes. By behaving as they did, they were seeking to express certain things about themselves and offering observers a violent commentary on their reactions to modern Italian life rather than pursuing concrete political objectives.

Yet there were elements of continuity between the two periods. First, there was the matter of milieu, what Italians refer to as *ambiente*. In both periods prominent neo-Fascist terrorists were drawn to violence from backgrounds in the Italian Social Movement, the party political manifestation of neo-Fascism. The gap between the MSI's ideology and its political performance in Parliament and elsewhere seems to have evoked disenchantment. In addition, for the neo-Fascist foot soldiers, the youth who were attracted to rightist violence, newspaper accounts emphasize that there were certain neighborhoods in the major cities, e.g., Monte Verde in Rome and Piazza San Babila in Milan, from which large numbers of the recruits came.[47] Indeed, one could do worse than to consider these recruits as members of politicized youth gangs replete with local hangouts and distinctive ways of dress and behavior.

Last, the neo-Fascist terrorist groups were bound together by a set of ideas. These conceptions were given various forms of expression in the two periods, but they had in common a rejection of economic self-interest and other materialistic premises of middle class life. These notions were to be transcended by the higher and more spiritually satisfying appeals of action, adventure and heroism.

Notes

1. Marino Regni, "Labor Unions, Industrial Action and Politics," in Peter Lange and Sidney Tarrow (eds.), *Italy in Transition* (London: Frank Cass & Co., LTD., 1980) pp. 49–66.

2. See for example Giuseppe Gaddi, *Neofascismo in Europa* (Milan: La Pietra, 1974) pp. 13–43; Petra Rosenbaum, *Il nuovo fascismo* (Milan: Feltrinelli, 1975) pp. 217–225.

3. See for example, Luigi Gennaro, Giudice Istruttore, Ordinanza/Sentenza N/ 568680A against the members of the neo-Fascist Third Position, (Tribunale di Roma, Ufficio Istruzione, 1980).

4. Ann Jellamo, "J. Evola, il pensatore della tradizione," in Franco Ferraresi (ed.), La destra radicale (Milan: Feltrinelli, 1984) pp. 215-247.

5. Patrizia Guerra and Marco Revelli (eds.) "Bibliografia essenziale per la conoscenza della nuova destra italiana," in Fascismo Oggi: nuova destra e cultura reazionaria negli anni ottanta (Cuneo: Istituto Storico della Resistenza, 1983) pp. 423-426.

6. Giorgio Freda, La disintegrazione del sistema (Padua: Edizioni AR, 1969) pp. 1-7.

7. Julius Evola, Il mito del sangue (Milan: Editore Hoepli, 1942) pp. 1-6.

8. On the development of these ideas see, Franco Ferraresi, "I Referimento teorico-dottrinali della destra radicale," Questione Giustizia 11:4 (1983) pp. 881-892; Franco Ferraresi, "Da Evola a Freda: le dottrine della destra radicale fino al 1977," in Franco Ferraresi (ed.), La destra radicale op. cit., pp. 13-41. On Romualdi see, Pino Romualdi (ed.), L'Italiano: Adriano Romualdi a dieci anni dalla sua scomparsa 24 (February, 1984) ad passim.

9. Quoted in Giulio Salierno, Autobiografia di un picchiatore fascista (Turin: Einaudi, 1976) p. 88.

10. Quoted in Ferraresi, "La destra eversiva," in Ferraresi (ed.), op. cit., p. 70.

11. "Radiografia del fascismo romano," Rinascita 29:11 (1972) pp. 18-20; also Gaddi, op. cit., p. 34.

12. Ruggero Zangrandi, Inchiesta sul SIFAR (Rome: Editori Riuniti, 1970) pp. 70-76.

13. Daniele Barberi, Agenda nera (Rome: Coines Edizioni, 1976) pp. 94-99.

14. Ricciotti Lazzero, La Decima Mas (Milan: Rizzoli, 1984) pp. 9-42.

15. Giampaolo Pansa, Borghese mi ha detto (Milan: Palazzi, 1971) pp. 42-43.

16. Marco Sassano, La politica delle strage (Padua: Marsilio, 1972) pp. 39-47.

17. Marco Fini and Andrea Barberi, Valpreda (Milan: Feltrinelli, 1972) pp. 102-104.

18. Cesare De Simone, La pista nera (Rome: Riuniti, 1972) pp. 38-42.

19. Sergio Turone, Storia del sindicato in Italia (Bari: Laterza, 1975) pp. 488-499.

20. For a chronological account of neo-Fascist violence in Milan leading up to Piazza Fontana see Luigi Majocchi (ed.) Rapporto sulla violenza fascista in Lombardia (Rome: Cooperative scrittori, 1975) pp. 15-21.

21. La Stampa (February 18 and 19, 1970) p. 2.

22. Guido Lorenzon, Teste a carico (Milan: Mondadori, 1976) pp. 33-76.

23. Vittorio Berraccetti, "Aspetti e problemi del terrorismo di destra," Questione Giustizia 2:4 (1983) pp. 870-871.

24. Fabrizio D'Agostini, Reggio Calabria (Milan: Feltrinelli, 1972) p. 19.

25. La Stampa (April 24, 1970) p. 1., and "La Stampa (May 23, 1970) p. 11.

26. Barberi, op. cit., pp. 193-198; Tina Anselmi, Il complotto di Licio Gelli, a report by the president of the parliamentary investigatory committee on Propaganda Due reprinted L'Espresso (May 20, 1984) pp. 37-38.

27. On this matter see the report of Franco Restiveo, the interior minister, to the Senate of the Republic, Atti parlamentari 22 (February 25, 1971) V legislatura, seduta 420, pp. 21-325-21-333.

28. On these themes see Mario Tedeschi, *Destra nazionale* (Rome: Edizioni del Borghese, 1972); Armando Plebe, *Il libretto della destra* (Milan: Edizioni del Borghese); and Giorgio Almirante, *La strategia del terrorismo* (Rome: SAIPEM, 1974).

29. *La Stampa* (November 11, 1973) p. 2., (January 12, 1974) p. 9, (January 22, 1974) p. 11., and (February 23, 1974) p. 9.

30. Roberto Chiarini and Paolo Corsini, *Da Salo a Piazza Della Loggia* (Milan: Franco Angelli, 1983) pp. 311–344.

31. Borraccetti, *op. cit.*, p. 871.

32. Giancarlo Scarpari, "Il processo per la strage dell'Italicus," in *Questione Giustizia op. cit.*, pp. 893–911.

33. La corte di assise di appello di Firenze, *Sentenza* (November 11, 1977); and *Sentenza* (April 9, 1976) pp. 2–4.

34. *La Stampa* (May 31, 1974) p. 1.

35. *Ibid.*, p. 1.

36. *La Stampa* (November 8, 1973) p. 9.

37. Ferraresi, "La destra eversiva," *op. cit.*, pp. 72–74.

38. La corte di assise di appello di Firenze, *Sentenza* (December 12, 1978) pp. 5–18.

39. Pier Luigi Vigna, "L'Omicidio del Magistrato Vittorio Occorsio: i processi e alcune riflessioni," *Questione Giustizia, op. cit.*, pp. 913–933.

40. Thomas Sheehan, "Italy: Terror on The Right," *New York Review of Books* 27:21 (1981) pp. 23–26; Marco Revelli, "La nuova destra," in Ferraresi (ed.), *op. cit.*, pp. 119–214; Giorgio Galli, "La componente magica della cultura di destra," in Quazza (ed.), *op. cit.*, pp. 279–286.

41. Giancarlo Capaldo et. al., "L'evresione di destra.

42. *Ibid.*, p. 955.

43. Marco Nozza, "'Quex': spontaneismo o progetto nazional-rivoluzionario," in Quazza (ed.), *op. cit.*, pp. 267–277.

44. *Corriere della Sera* (October 6, 1982) p. 26; Claudio Gerino, "Ora stiamo braccando i latitanti dei NAR," *La Repubblica* (October 7, 1982) p. 10.

45. Franco Coppola, "Bologna, 4 ergastoli per l'omicidio Amato," *La Repubblica* (April 6, 1984) p. 12.

46. *La Repubblica* (August 7, 1980) p. 2.

47. *La Stampa* (April 22, 1973) p. 1.

RED TERRORISM: THE REVOLUTIONARIES, 1969-1984

4

Retrieving the Revolutionary Idea

If neo-Fascist violence dominated Italian terrorism during the late 1960s and the first half of the 70s, it is clear that between the second half of the latter decade and the early 1980s, political violence was largely the work of groups professing leftist goals and objectives, ones intended to achieve the triumph of the Italian working class by means of revolution. In examining the origins of these revolutionary organizations, and the ideas from which they derived their inspiration, it is necessary to do more than refer the reader to the works of Bakunin, Marx and Lenin or their contemporary explicators outside Italy.

To understand where the revolutionary terrorists came from and the goals they sought to achieve, it is necessary to trace the origins of the New left movements in which many of them became politically conscious and of the ideas which led to the formation of these movements. Their origins are to be found in a set of small circulation journals written and largely read by left-wing intellectuals.

The stimulus for their publication were events that occurred on the international scene in 1956. That was the year of Khrushchev's secret speech at the USSR's twentieth party congress in which he revealed Stalin's enormous crimes. It was also the year of the Soviet Union's military repression of the Hungarian uprising. These events had a profound impact on many young left-wing intellectuals. For most of them, Stalin had been a revered figure, a revolutionary leader who had led the fight against fascism. And the Soviet regime over which he had presided had been considered by these Socialist and Communist intellectuals as a suitable model for Italy.

53

Among the consequences of these disillusioning events was a need to publicly rethink their understanding of the world. The means by which these intellectuals sought to express themselves was through the publication of articles in journals explicitly created for this purpose.

The central themes running through articles published in the little magazines *Quaderni Rossi*, *Quaderni Piacentini*, *Classe Operaio*, *Scienza Operaia* and others were ones that stressed the need to develop a strategy for the achievement of socialism in Italy that rejected both reformism and Stalinsim.[1] The perspective of writers like Antonio Negri, Adriano Sofri, Sergio Bologna and Raniero Panzieri began from the premise that socialist revolution was necessary in Italy as elsewhere. Their dream was to complete the unfulfilled revolutionary objectives of the Resistance and, by so doing, liberate the country's working class from capitalist exploitation. Stalinism, with its connotation of bureaucratic hierarchy and state terrorism, was rejected. Reformism, on the other hand, represented capitulation to the capitalist system. Peaceful coexistence with imperialism was also regarded with disdain. The links between Italy's historic left, the Socialists and Communists, and the working class, particularly the new "mass" workers up from the South, had been severed. And although they did not use the term, these Marxist protestants saw the traditional leftist parties and unions as susceptible to the 'iron law of oligarchy' with interests to pursue that had become detached from those of the workers. There was a need therefore for new forms of collective behavior, some organizational, some spontaneous, that could express the genuine needs of the Italian working class.

From the early to the mid-1960s, these intellectuals were in search of examples around the world which might be applied to the Italian situation. Some saw models worthy of emulation in China under Mao or in the Castroite experience in Cuba and related developments elsewhere in Latin America. Others took note of events occurring in the United States, notably the civil rights struggle and the evolving anti-war movement. Commentaries on the meaning of these developments were combined with reinterpretations of Marx, Luxemburg, Trotsky and along with the writings of earlier Italian revolutionaries.

It was out of this need to retrieve a revolutionary tradition and assign it a place in modern Italy that the New Left was formed. But was it conceivable that such highly abstract thoughts could be translated into some form of plausible action? After all, other western democracies abounded with little magazines of their own in which similar thoughts were being expressed at approximately the same time. How could such views capture a mass appeal and lead to the organization of new movements that would somehow transform them into practice?

Growth of the New Left and the Genesis
of Revolutionary Terrorist Groups

First of the new groups to be formed from the little magazines was the Communist party of Italy Marxist-Leninist (PC d'I [M-L]). Created in Livorno (which had been the site, not coincidentally, of the founding of the Italian Communist party in 1921) in 1966, its program asserted that armed struggle is a universal principle of revolution from which there are no exceptions.[2] The party's behavior would be guided, its leaders claimed, by the ideals of the Communist Manifesto, the Paris Commune and the Maoist achievements in China. Its attitude towards the massive Italian Communist party and the question of revolution parallel Mao's judgments concerning the domestic and foreign policy heresies of the Soviet leadership.

Within several years of its creation, this new Communist party suffered a number of ideologically based factional disputes and scissions. Our interest in the party derives from the fact that radical students at the University of Trento, an institution established in 1962 for the study of the social sciences, became involved in it. Among the Trento students who joined the party (in 1968) were Renato Curcio and Margherita Cagol, shortly to found their own organization, the Red Brigades.[3]

A second group to serve as an incubator for revolutionary terrorism was organized, like the Communist party of Italy Marxist-Leninist, in Tuscany in 1966–67. Organized by writers for *Quaderni Rossi*, it first took the name Worker Power (*Potere Operaio*). Its initial adherents were drawn from Pisa, Livorno and Massa. Some were students at the University of Pisa, others were workers at small factories in these Tuscan communities. Adriano Sofri and its other founders defined Worker Power as in the tradition of the Third International. Editorials in its publication demanded the elimination of salary differentials among workers and advanced other worker specific proposals. However, these statements also proclaimed the need to extend the workers' struggle beyond the factory gates in order to stimulate revolutionary sentiment. Parallels between Vietnam and the Italian situation were drawn. In 1968, as the student protests exploded, Worker Power's leaders discussed the prospects of making the parallel something more than a literary metaphor. Calling for an "armed struggle of long duration", they decided to attempt the formation of a nationwide organization. In 1969 Worker Power's leaders, now active in Milan, held meetings with members of several other newly formed worker and student groups. These were merged to form the Struggle Continues (*Lotta Continua* O LC). LC was to become one of the major New Left movements active in Italy, an organization that at the height of its popularity would have over 100,000 members with sections in all the major cities.[4] Later still, dissident LC militants would create a succession of revolutionary terrorist groups—as we shall see.

The story of Giangiacomo Feltrinelli, the multi-millionaire Milanese publisher, has been told often. A Marxist, Feltrinelli had become enthralled by the victory of the Castro insurgency in Cuba as well as the efforts of other guerrilla bands to produce similar results in other Latin American nations. (He visited the French Marxist Regis Debray in Bolivia in 1967 and sought to aid Che Guevara's ill-fated operations in that country.) He was so taken by these experiences that after returning to Italy in 1967, Feltrinelli concluded that his own country might be ripe for such adventures. In his mind the island of Sardinia represented the closest Italian equivalent to the Sierra Maestra. Unfortunately, from his point of view, the Sardinian bandits with whom he made contact did not share this enthusiasm. After again visiting Castro in 1968, one of several trips to Cuba, Feltrinelli returned to Italy with his revolutionary fervor undiminished. The parallel between Vietnam and Italy occurred to him as it had to the Worker Power's editorialists. To this shared vision of a counter attack against the forces of imperialism, he added a concern with the danger of a right-wing coup d'état in Italy. Various accounts of the 1968–69 period portrayed Feltrinelli as a man who had become obsessed with this possibility.[5] As we have seen, this fear of a neo-Fascist conspiracy was not without its foundation in reality; the neo-Fascists had just such a scheme in mind. The irony is that the right-wing military officers and neo-Fascist leaders who concocted it were themselves obsessed by fear of another conspiratorial design, a Communist one. If there was ever a self-fulfilling prophecy at work this was it. Each side was beginning to conjure up the other.

What should be the appropriate response to the right-wing threat? Feltrinelli's answer, after the Piazza Fontana bombing had confirmed his worst fears, was the formation of a revolutionary and clandestine organization, the Partisan Action Group (GAP), a name taken from World War II resistance movement's fight against Fascism. For Feltrinelli the need for a renewal of that struggle was manifest. This time, however, the new partisans would not stop with defeating Fascism, they would also make a revolution.

The political traditions of Tuscany and the Veneto regions of Italy are very different. An historic center of anarchism and long a stronghold of the Communist party, Tuscany, as we have just seen, was also the area from which LC and PC d'I (M-L) were to develop and then spread north to Turin and Milan. The Veneto, in the northeastern part of the country, had no such revolutionary credentials. It was a region which by tradition was largely Catholic and conservative. Yet it was also in the Veneto that another New Left movement was to be formed, one which would later produce its own cadres of revolutionary terrorists.[6]

In the early 1960s dissident socialist and Catholic intellectuals like Antonio Negri and Mario Tronti, many of them professors or students at the University of Padua, began publishing a series of short-lived little magazines, journals focused on the meaning of revolution after the events of 1956. As in Tuscany, some of the intellectuals saw the need to foster an organization which could serve as an expression for their views. Contacts were made with workers at the petro-chemical plants in Porto Marghera near Venice. Some of the workers were responsive, particularly those in plants without a strong trade union presence. The intellectuals from Padua and the industrial workers established a local organization called Worker Power (POTOP). This group, in conjunction with similarly minded ones in Turin, Ivrea and Milan, formed a unified movement in September 1969 which also took the name Worker Power.

As one of its early members described it, POTOP had more nervous energy than ideology. Nonetheless, its leaders, Negri along with Oreste Scalzone and Franco Piperno, considered it to be a nominally Leninist body. Negri and the other ideologues counseled workers not to get caught up in trade unionist tactics and indeed recommended that they reject the work ethic entirely.[7] Instead POTOP's leaders argued in favor of the "refusal of work" in all its modern industrial forms as the way by which the capitalist system could be brought down. In place of the organization and discipline inherent in the trade unionist approach to industrial conflict, POTOP stressed that workers' "spontaneity" should be the central tactic, a notion rather distant from what Lenin had had in mind.[8] By the early 1970s, POTOP's membership was to number several thousand, some of whom were to later follow the path of clandestinity and terrorism.

In addition to its Fascist and Communist, variously defined, components, the tradition of political terrorism in Italy also has involved a strong anarchist strand. As we have observed, terrorism committed to further anarchist principles was particularly prevalent at the end of the 19th and beginning of the 20th centuries. But what of anarchism in the contemporary setting?

Anarchism did not disappear with the advent of Italy's postwar democratic regime. During the 1950s an array of anarchist groups were organized in Livorno, Carrara and Genoa. There was also a national federation. By the early 1960s, Milan had its Gaetano Bresci Group and a Sacco and Vanzetti Circle.[9] In 1965 these groups participated in anti-Vietnam War protests. The new anarchists were attracted to the satiric tactics exhibited by the Dutch Provos in this period, as well as by the concept of direct democracy advocated by French, German and American student radicals. Later, during the crucial years of 1968–69, anarchists participated in the mass student and worker protests. All this, however, was still a far cry from terrorism.

It is true that the anarchists, Pinelli and Valpreda, were used as foils in the Piazza Fontana bombing; yet as is known now, it was neo-Fascists who were responsible for the massacre. But to what extent was there an authentic anarchist role in the contemporary terrorist episode? The answer is that anarchists played a role but not an especially significant one. In May 1973, an individual anarchist, Gianfranco Bertoli, hurled a hand grenade in front of police headquarters in Milan as an act of revenge, so he said, for the death of his fellow anarchist Pinelli in that building. Four people were killed as a result of his gesture.[10] (Bertoli, whose biography included 22 previous arrests—one for shooting a pistol in school at the age of 16, apparently acted alone.) But so far as anarchist group violence is concerned, there is not much to report. In the mid-1970s some acts of political terrorism were committed by Revolutionary Action, an anarchist band organized by Gianfranco Faina, a former professor of political science at the University of Genoa. Faina had been the author of articles in *Quaderni Rossi* and *Classe Operaio*, an experience he shared with other revolutionary terrorist writers.[11]

The principal legacy that the historic anarchist movement bequeathed to the recent generation of left-wing terrorists was more theoretical than organizational. As we shall see, the tactics of the early Red Brigades and other Communist groups were built around the principle of the "exemplary action," the idea that by committing an act of violence against a single target identified as an enemy of the workers, the deed would show others the way. The tactic was of anarchist, not Leninist, origin. But as a group professing the historic ideology, anarchists did not count much in the recent terrorist episode.

An important factor to bear in mind is the impact of the 1968–69 crisis in the development of left-wing terrorism. Before the student and worker explosion, there existed a collection of small journals whose writers were committed to retrieving the idea of armed revolution as a concept that many, including the Communists, thought implausible or inapplicable in advanced industrialized societies. These intellectuals began to act on their beliefs. Small groups were created to transform these views into action. In other circumstances, this is likely where things would have stopped. No doubt, debates would have occurred over the failure to achieve a revolution. Factions would have emerged over arcane ideological interpretations. All of this would likely have led to nothing. The social and economic environment would have provided a reality test for the revolutionaries which should have led them to the conclusion that a revolutionary situation did not exist.

But instead of reaching this sort of dead end, the revolutionaries confronted a situation in 1968–69 that must have exceeded their wildest expectations. Hundreds of thousands of students were caught up in wave upon wave of protests. Even better, the student uprising was followed by militant worker actions in the northern cities. The workers were beginning to act like the

Left v. right (extreme positions.)

proletarians on whose behalf the Communist revolution was supposed to be made, or so it seemed. Many of the workers, younger ones especially, were responsive to the kinds of appeals from students and New Left revolutionaries to which their counterparts in the United States, West Germany and most other western democracies were immune. The events of 1968–69 provided the revolutionaries with hope and a large clientele receptive to their ideas. What more could they ask for?

The answer is Fascism. Fascism existed not only as a metaphor with which to berate the wielders of economic and political power, nor did it exist solely as a hated symbol out of the Italian past, Fascism existed as a concrete phenomenon. There was the MSI, New Order, et al. Furthermore, this neo-Fascism apparently had links to elements within the bourgeois state. If ever there was an enemy to be fought, this was it.

The initial result of this radicalization of the environment was, as we have seen, the formation and expansion of the New Left movements; POTOP and LC were joined by Worker Vanguard (AO) and Manifesto, a group of Communist party dissidents. At this stage of their development, the new movements were committed to making a revolution in Italy, but not through acts of individual terrorism. Their route to revolution encompassed the transformation of their student and worker sympathizers into a vanguard which would proceed, in Leninist fashion, to raise the revolutionary consciousness of the millions. The means by which this task was to be accomplished involved the instruments of mass mobilization: parades, demonstrations, pamphlets and loudspeakers in front of factory gates, as well as recruitment campaigns within the plants themselves.

But some who had been affected by the events of 1968–69 chose an alternative route to revolution. This was the path of the urban guerrilla, and it was to be followed, at first, by Feltrinelli's GAP, a related band called 22 October, and an organization which would endure into the 1980s, the Red Brigades (BR).

The story of *22 October* is a brief one.[12] In 1970–71 Mario Rossi, a thirty year old taxidermist, former Communist and a man with Maoist views, attracted a small group of followers in Genoa and obtained a handful of weapons from a sympathetic gun shop owner. Rossi and his band then committed a series of "proletarian expropriations" and nocturnal assaults on police stations. In the course of the attempted kidnapping of a Genovese businessman they managed to kill their victim. In 1971 the police arrested Renato Rinaldi, a member of the group. He proceeded to tell investigators all they wished to know about 22 October. Rossi and his several dozen followers were than taken into custody; in 1973 they were tried and convicted for their crimes.

The state prosecutor in Genoa who led the investigation of 22 October, Mario Sossi, was a man who had been a member of an MSI youth group as a young student.[13] When this fact became known, it provided the New left movements with an irresistible opportunity to portray the members of 22 October as victims of a political trial conducted by a neo-Fascist counterrevolutionary on behalf of a capitalist state.

Genoa was also the site of another incident which attracted considerable publicity. On April 16, 1970, viewers of the state television channel in that city had the audio portion of their transmission interrupted by an announcement from a private source. The unexpected voice announced the formation of a new organization, GAP of Feltrinelli's inspiration. Later, more conventional means were used to communicate the message that other GAP units were beginning operations in Turin, Milan and other northern cities. The objective of GAP was to launch a counterattack against the forces of fascism and repression that were on the verge of taking control of the state. The situation in Italy, as defined by Feltrinelli and his followers, paralleled that of the country in 1943–45. The fact that northern Italy in 1970 was not occupied by Nazis and Fascists (Turin had a Socialist mayor) made no difference. The need was the same. GAP committed itself to a course of clandestine organization and urban political violence.

Measured by the amount of violence it inflicted, GAP did not amount to very much. A few bombs were exploded and several fires set. One person, Carlo Saronio, ostensibly a member of the band, was kidnapped and killed by his own colleagues. Feltrinelli managed to kill himself while trying to plant an explosive charge on an electric power line near Milan in April 1972.

The interest in Feltrinelli, aside from his enormous wealth and personal eccentricities, derives from the relationships he developed with other revolutionaries who had become committed to the armed struggle. Before his self-inflicted death, Feltrinelli had sought to ally GAP with other revolutionary organizations beginning their operations in northern Italy. Whether or not Feltrinelli's behavior was determined or conditioned by the Cubans, Czechs and Soviets, as has been alleged, remains unresolved. In domestic terms, it has been proven in Italian courts that he did meet with Renato Curcio, a founder and early leader of the Red Brigades.[14] Records of these meetings, as well as his encounters with other BR members, were later uncovered by the police in a BR hideout. It is true, also, that after Feltrinelli's death, some GAP members became Red Brigadists.

But observers who assign Feltrinelli a central role in the promotion of left-wing terrorism place particular importance on his meetings with the leaders of POTOP: Negri, Scalzone, Piperno and others. The fact that such meetings did occur now seems beyond dispute. The testimony of the repentant terrorist Carlo Fiorini, a Milanese high school teacher, has been admitted in several court proceedings.[15] Also, documentary evidence, in the form of correspondence between Feltrinelli and POTOP's leaders was found by the authorities among Feltrinelli's files and later introduced as evidence in the trial of Negri and the others. In one of these communications, Feltrinelli advocated the formation of a common command structure for the revolutionary forces emerging in the North and expressed his willingness to finance the project. While his money was accepted, not all of the proposals were. Piperno reacted by telling Feltrinelli that his creation of GAP as an anti-Fascist guerrilla group lacked any understanding of the Italian working class (of which neither were members). Italy, according to Piperno, was only at the initial phase of its revolution; it was hardly ready for civil war. Nonetheless, after Feltrinelli's death arms, money and militants from GAP passed into the hands of POTOP as well as the BR.

The origins of the Red Brigades are well known by now.[16] In 1969 radical students from the University of Trento, led by Curcio and his wife Margherita Cagol, moved to Milan. There they encountered radicalized workers from autonomous (non-unionized) groups at the Pirelli tire plant and other factories. In conjunction with young ex-Communists from Reggio Emilia, they formed the Metropolitan Political Collective. The group began *Proletarian Left*, a publication committed to the radicalization of the working class. *Proletarian Left* and another short-lived periodical, *New Resistance*, published interviews with Palestinian guerrillas and Latin American revolutionaries along with the revolutionary views of the Metropolitan Collectivists. The message was the necessity of armed struggle.

The publications were short-lived. Their editors had decided to put the words into practice. In 1971 Curcio and other members of the new BR embarked on a course of armed actions in Milan and the other industrial cities of northern Italy. By contrast to Feltrinelli, the BR had no illusions about partisan operations in the mountains or a new Cuba in the Mediterranean. As they saw it, the struggle would be in the great metropolitan centers where the contradictions of capitalism were most apparent and where their prospective clientele, the workers, lived.

The initial tactic was that of armed propaganda. Acts of violence, at first against property and then against people, were directed against "enemies" of the workers. These exemplary actions were followed by copious communiqués in which the BR explained why it had acted against a particular target.

At first the BR operated on the basis of a combination of these covert attacks and the open distribution of explanatory propaganda by its members in the plants and factories where it hoped to win recruits. However, in 1972 the police arrested a number of BR militants as they were handing out the organization's communiqués. This led the BR leadership to rethink its approach. They concluded, unsurprisingly, that the mixture of open propagandizing and recruiting with covert violence would not work. The alternative was total, or near total, clandestinity. Accordingly, the BR introduced a distinction between "regulars" who would work as full-time revolutionaries and "irregulars" who would try to conduct normal lives and provide external support for the clandestine regulars.[17]

The support of revolutionaries leading clandestine lives is expensive. They need bases from which to operate, weapons with which to conduct their business, as well as food, clothing and shelter. For the most part these needs were met by means of "self-financing," the revolutionary expression for theft. Support also required the development of a relatively extensive organization.

At this stage of its evolution, the BR formed its organizational apparatus. Each city—Milan, Turin, Genoa—where a sufficient number of regulars could be recruited, had a BR "column". The columns were then subdivided into brigades for purposes of conducting terrorist operations. Parallel to these structures were various "fronts" for the irregulars: a logistical front (with responsibility for the acquisition of arms, bases, false license plates and documents), a front for the major factories and a mass front. Both the columns and fronts were directed by an executive committee, composed in this formative period by the BR's founders.

As this account suggests, the BR quickly became something more than a small band of revolutionaries operating in Milan. It was able to attract to its "historic nucleus" adherents from other northern cities, at least some of whom came from working class backgrounds.

For the first two years of its existence, the BR's violence was limited to attacks on property; no people were harmed. Then on March 3, 1972 a manager at the Sit-Siemens electrical company in Milan was kidnapped. He was then subjected to "proletarian justice." The businessman was subjected to a trial in which he was condemned for crimes against the working class, photographed in a proletarian prison and released uninjured.[18] After this widely publicized accomplishment, the BR kidnapped and dispensed proletarian justice to several more businessmen along with a few union officials it accused of colluding with them. Nonetheless, by the end of 1973 no one had as yet been killed or seriously injured by the BR. Its actions had been attention getting, yet not lethal.

Nineteen seventy-four was the year of the Brescia and Italicus massacres, the *Rosa dei venti* scheme and the Communist party's proposal of an "historic compromise" with the Christian Democrats to rule Italy. It was also the year, not coincidentally, in which the BR widened its horizons and changed tactics. As the BR defined it, the situation was one in which the Italian state had entered a profound crisis which would take it in an even more repressive and reactionary direction than had been the case previously.

In this situation we must accept war. . . . We must transform the crisis into the first moments of armed proletarian power, of the armed struggle for communism. Historic compromise or armed proletarian power: this is the choice that comrades today must make.[19]

The BR was committing itself to strike at the heart of the state.

The first manifestation of the new, more ambitious strategy was the kidnapping on April 18, 1974 of Mario Sossi, the state prosecutor in Genoa, who had investigated the 22 October group. This was an act that took the BR away from the factories and exemplary actions against private businesses and onto a course of confrontation with the state.

In memoirs published after his release, Sossi recalls the experience of his captivity. In this account he mentions the books his captors gave him to further his re-education. Beyond the obligatory Marxist-Leninist volumes, these included works about the Italian Resistance, an experience the BR militants treated in almost reverential terms. Sossi observed: "I know very well that the Communist partisans are the historical model used by the Red Brigades."[20] In a conversation, one of his captors described the BR as the embodiment of the revolutionary Communist tradition in Italy, a tradition discarded by the revisionist PCI. The Palestine Liberation Organization was another source of inspiration for the kidnappers, as Sossi relates it. PLO attacks at Maalot and other cities in Israel were examples of what the BR intended to do in Italy.

In fact, what the BR did in Sossi's case was demand an exchange of prisoners. In exchange for this release they demanded freedom for members of the October 22 group. If the government failed to comply, then Sossi would be executed. The kidnapping produced an enormous amount of nationwide publicity. Thousands of police were committed to uncovering Sossi's whereabouts, without effect. And although the government refused to negotiate, the DC leader, Amintore Fanfani, made a speech in which he said that Sossi's life must be saved. Pope Paul appealed to the BR not to kill their captive.

On May 23, 1974 Sossi was released, but only after the chief state prosecutor in Genoa, Francesco Coco, persuaded an appeals court to release the October 22 group on what amounted to a technicality. But after Sossi was free, Coco convinced the court to reverse its decision, a doublecross the BR would remember.

Within a few weeks of this episode, another BR brigade entered the provincial headquarters of the MSI in Padua and murdered two neo-Fascist officials they found inside. It was the first time the BR had killed. But the organization had to pay a price for these murders and the Sossi kidnapping. The authorities made a determined effort to track down the terrorists. Accordingly, by the end of 1974, numerous BR militants had been arrested, including most members of the organization's executive: Curcio, Alfredo Buonavita, Alberto Franceschini, Prospero Gallinari and others. Bases and hide-outs all over northern Italy were uncovered and an enormous quantity of documents and weapons seized.

Nineteen seventy-five did not bring the BR any better luck. It is true that Curcio was able to break out of prison and that the BR conducted a number of successful operations against Christian Democratic offices and politicians, but the defeats outweighed these victories. Margherita Cagol was killed during a shootout with the police during a kidnapping attempt. There were additional arrests, and, at the beginning of 1976, Curcio was recaptured. On the surface it appeared as if the BR had run its course.

But the BR was not the only revolutionary terrorist group active in Italy in these years. There was also the Nuclei of Armed Proletarians (NAP). If the BR's origins are to be found in the encounter between radical students and militant workers in Milan, the genesis of NAP derives from the meeting of two analogous forces: revolutionaries from the new left LC and inmates in Italian prisons.[21]

In the early 1970s, LC's position concerning the BR and GAP was one of sympathy, not emulation. Officially, the movement favored mass action and general conflict, not isolated attacks by clandestine groups. However, there were some members of *Lotta Continua* who had reached other conclusions.

As with so many of Italy's institutions, its prison system had entered a period of crisis in the early 1970s. There had been a series of riots inside several of the country's largest prisons, protests aimed at improving conditions. These disturbances led LC to create a prison commission to investigate these conditions. The product of this private inquiry was the publication of a tract, *Liberate All the Wretched of The Earth*, whose authors reached the conclusion that the inmates, like the country's working class, were the victims of capitalist exploitation. And as with the latter, so too with the prisoners: there was a profound need for liberation by revolutionary means.

During 1974 an effort was made to transform this judgment into violent practice. Disaffected members of the prison commission, along with other LC activists in Naples, largely university students and ex-inmates who had been politicized by their radical well-wishers, combined to organize the Nuclei of Armed Proletarians (NAP).

As an organization, NAP was a far cruder formation than the BR, and its existence was a far more ephemeral one than that of the latter (its existence spanned approximately two years). But the operations NAP undertook resembled those of the Red Brigades. There were initial efforts at proletarian expropriation, i.e., bank robbery, attacks on MSI offices and the kidnapping of a prominent jurist.[22] Yet NAP, led by such former LC figures as Giovanni Gentile Schiavone and Pietro Sofia, was never able to develop an effective organizational structure outside Naples. Attempts were made to establish groups in Florence and Milan but without success. Rome was more promising. For a brief period in 1975–76, a NAP group was able to establish itself in the capital and to do some damage, including the killing of the head of the anti-terrorism police unit in the city.[23]

Because of the willingness of NAP members, particularly those drawn from its contingent of subproletarian professional criminals, to talk to the police when they were arrested, practically all the major figures in the Neapolitan NAP were caught by the police in 1975. And in 1976, its bases in Rome were discovered and most of its militants were apprehended. One leader, Antonio Lo Musica, a former Sicilian bandit, was shot dead on the Spanish Steps when he pulled a gun in response to a routine police inquiry.[24]

With the demise of NAP, for all intents and purposes, and the arrest of the Red Brigades' "historic nucleus" it appeared by 1976 that revolutionary terrorism was on the verge of collapse. Unfortunately, though, the story does not end here. The second half of the 70s was characterized by the revitalization of left-wing terrorism and a vast increase in the amount and deadliness of the violence for which it was responsible.

The Second Explosion

On May 17, 1976 members of the BR's "historic nucleus" went on trial in Turin. In response to the charges against them, they denied the court's jurisdiction, and not only refused the court's appointed defense attorneys, but threatened with death any bourgeois lawyers who dared represent them.[25] The BR founders wished to defend themselves. The trial proceedings were suspended until the appellate court in Rome could rule on this demand. When the trial resumed on June 9, the defendants appeared jubilant. Although their appeal had been denied, another event had occurred during the suspension that gave them cause to celebrate. Francesco Coco, the state prosecutor in Genoa—the man who had doublecrossed them after the release of Mario Sossi—had been assassinated. Coco and his bodyguard had been gunned down on a street in Genoa by a BR brigade. It was apparent that the Red Brigades and revolutionary terrorism in Italy had not come to an end. What had happened?

In a general sense the answer is that support for revolutionary terrorism had grown, not diminished. This expansion was fed, in no small measure, by defecting members of the extra-parliamentary new left movements, POTOP and LC in particular.

Formally POTOP had disbanded itself as an open above ground political organization in 1972. Part of its membership was restructured as Organized Worker Autonomy (AO), still another open political formation, with "collectives" in major cities, which began to engage in various forms of street protest and often violent agitation. But another segment of POTOP's several thousand members had found their way into the Red Brigades.[26]

Similar events occurred within *Lotta Continua*, the movement from which NAP's leaders had come. From 1973 there was a conflict within LC between a faction which advocated following a democratic path and providing conditional support for the Communist party, and another group that advocated the armed struggle. At the 1974 LC congress in Rimini, approximately 150 of the movement's militants walked out in protest against the majority's decision to support the PCI in that year's regional elections. The defectors were led by members of LC's Lenin Circle in Sesto San Giovanni, an industrial suburb of Milan and longtime bastion of Communist support.[27] Likeminded groups of LC dissidents existed in Turin, Bergamo and Florence as well. During 1975 members of the Sesto San Giovanni group began to commit acts of political violence using a variety of labels, most frequently that of *Senza Tregua* (Without Truce). Former members of POTOP in Milan were also attracted to the new group.

In 1976 LC participated in the national election campaign as part of an alliance of New Left groups, as the Democratic Proletarian party. Expectations were high, but the party was unable to win more than 2 per cent of the vote. As a consequence of this profoundly disillusioning electoral defeat, LC disintegrated. Worse, the election also permitted the hated Christian Democrats to return to power. For many of the LC revolutionaries, this was too much. As they saw it, the only option remaining for those committed to bringing about radical change in Italy was the violent one.

The product of these developments was Front Line (PL). This terrorist group was organized during 1976 by such former LC members as Carlo Donat Cattin, the son of a Christian Democratic cabinet minister, and Professor Corrado Marcetti of the University of Florence, along with other New Left revolutionaries from Milan, Turin, Bergamo and Florence. Front Line's founders were committed to the same revolutionary objectives as those of the BR. However, they wished to avoid the latter's obvious error, that of losing touch with the masses—a result , they believed, of the BR's excessive commitment to clandestinity. No group could act as a surrogate for the proletariat as the BR had attempted. Front Line, by contrast, would seek to stimulate the formation of a future proletarian army.[28]

As an organization, PL sought to establish contacts with the working class via the formation of above ground Proletarian Squads, units located in the major cities, and, incredibly as it may seem, by the setting up of a press office to handle communications with the public. So far as its terrorist or "military" operations were concerned, PL used small Firing Groups whose behavior was controlled by the leader of each PL organization active in the different cities. Yet as the PL's violent activities mounted over the next several years and despite the intent to avoid the BR's mistakes, it became an almost exclusively clandestine organization. The more terrorist violence it perpetrated, the more its plans for contacts with its presumed clientele became implausible.

The sort of violent attacks the PL committed, beginning in 1977, were different from the sporadic exemplary actions of the early Red Brigades. Instead, PL defined itself as waging full-scale campaigns against particularly hated sectors of Italian society and polity. The targets of these campaigns were the bourgeois press, the Christian Democratic party, the police and judiciary and real estate developers. For the most part, the campaigns amounted to nothing more than shooting selected representatives of these institutions.

Also in 1977, as the PL was launching these operations, the BR underwent another behavioral change. After undergoing a process of crisis, reassessment and reorganization, brought on by the arrest of most of its early leadership group, the BR's Strategic Direction, its national leadership group, committed the organization to a policy of not merely striking at the heart of the state, but of seeking to "disarticulate" it. The BR's new generation of leaders, such as Barbara Balzerani and Patrizio Peci as well as a few like Mario Moretti from the earlier generation who managed to evade capture, conceived the BR's ultimate goals to be susceptible to a far more "militarist" resolution than had their predecessors. And by disarticulating the state, they had in mind attacks on Christian Democratic leaders and intermediate level functionaries, trade union representatives, Communist party officers and various middle ranking members of the state bureaucracy.

Thus, by 1977 there were at work in the country two major revolutionary terrorist groups with clandestine or semi-clandestine organizational presences in most major cities, each of which were by now committed to carrying out continuous and massive campaigns of terrorist violence. But, in addition to the BR and PL, and to make matters worse, 1977 also saw the re-ignition of the kind of mass protest and street rioting that had characterized the 1968–69 period.

In February there were massive student protests staged at the University of Rome, ones involving a group called the Metropolitan Indians. These "Indians" jeered and heckled when Luciano Lama, the Communist trade union leader, appeared at the university to address a student gathering. Lama was prevented from speaking and his bodyguard had to lead him away, fearing for his safety.[29]

On March 11 a student and former member of LC was killed by the police during a demonstration at the University of Bologna. The students reacted to the shooting by shutting down the university and by causing sufficient violence in the rest of the city for its Communist mayor to call for police reinforcements.[30] These events set-off additional demonstrations in Milan, Padua and Rome as thousands of students took to the streets in solidarity with their Bolognese colleagues.

The Communist party and the major trade union federations responded to the renewal of mass protest by staging their own peaceful demonstrations, ones aimed at promoting a restoration of law and order. This reaction was perhaps symbolic of a growing and important division in Italian society. On the one hand, there were the Communists, administrators of the prosperous city of Bologna and on the verge of sharing power with the Christian Democrats at the national level. In addition, there were the trade union federations, many of whose members enjoyed job security, as well as insulation against the by now galloping inflation rate because of an escalator clause built into their labor contracts. On the other hand, there were hundreds of thousands of the intellectual unemployed, people who had prepared themselves at the universities for professional occupations in a job market that was already overcrowded. Furthermore, in the major cities there were masses of young people attending secondary schools whose future employment prospects appeared bleak, as well as many more young adults both out of school and in search of work. Finally, there was a large number of young women in rebellion against the sexually discriminatory values left over from the Italian past. This collection of the alienated provides us with a background against which we can view the events of the next several years.

First of all, there was the development of the so-called "diffuse" terrorism of AO.[31] The events in Rome, Bologna, Padua and Milan in the first part of 1977 were not totally spontaneous occurrences. The protests and violence had been amplified by members of Worker Autonomy active at these universities. Rather than a clandestine organization, AO was an "archipelago" of groups or collectives with their own publications, such as the journal *Rosso*, and even their own radio stations, such as Radio Sherwood in Padua. From 1977 the AO collectives engaged in a combination of open and large scale mass protest and surreptitious terrorist attacks using, for this purpose, a long list of group names and symbols. The extent to which there existed a degree of planning and coordination between the AO's operations and those of the clandestine BR and PL remains a matter of dispute. What is clear, however, is that the AO offensive against the Italian state coincided with an explosion of terrorist acts committed by the Red Brigades and Front Line.

By the middle of April 1977, *Panorama*, the weekly news magazine, published a cover story on terrorism under the headline: "We are in South America."[32] Carlo Rosella, the story's author, went on to compare the situation in Italy with that of Chile in 1973 immediately before the military *coup* against the Allende government. Despite the attempted parallel, Italy's democracy was to survive. Nonetheless, over the next several years, the country experienced an enormous wave of revolutionary terrorism, as groups from the BR, PL and smaller formations linked to AO conducted their campaigns against exponents of Italy's various public, and from their point of view, bourgeois and imperialist institutions.

According to figures published by the government, there were 2,128 separate terrorist attacks during 1977, almost twice the number of the previous year. Among the most frequent targets were political parties and their officials (there were 150 attacks on Christian Democratic offices alone), local police offices, schools, trade union branches, prisons and headquarters of large business firms. Forty-two policemen were listed among those killed by the terrorists in 1977.[33]

Naturally, not all these events can be described here, but a few are worth recounting. In April, Fulvio Croce, the 77 year old president of the lawyer's guild in Turin, was shot dead by BR members as he returned to his office from lunch. He was executed for having tried to provide defense attorneys for the BR leaders on trial in his community. In Genoa, a Communist party activist and worker at the Ansaldo plant was shot in the leg ("kneecapped") by another BR squad. The BR had concluded that he was a revisionist, a follower of Berlinguer, the PCI leader, and worse, had encouraged other workers to follow the same heretical line.[34]

These events and the more than 2,000 like them that occurred in 1977, led some to believe, not least of which was the BR leadership itself, that the authorities were confronted, not by a small number of terrorists belonging to a handful of clandestine organizations, but by an "armed party", a significant segment of the population that had decided to use guns rather than ballots to express their political views. In other words, by the end of 1977, there existed in Italy hundreds of revolutionary terrorists with thousands of supporters and well-wishers and, potentially, a mass constituency in the big cities responsive to the slogan, "neither with the state nor the BR."

Without doubt the most significant event in the BR's attempt to disarticulate the state began on March 16, 1978 when Aldo Moro, the former prime minister and pre-eminent Christian Democratic leader, was abducted. Moro was taken from his automobile on the Via Fani in Rome by a brigade from the BR Roman Column. This was done after they had killed his driver and police bodyguards. On May 10, 55 days later, Moro's body was found in the trunk of an abandoned car left in the middle of Rome, approximately halfway between the national headquarters of the DC and PCI.

The Red Brigades had managed to hold captive, for close to two months, one of Italy's most important postwar leaders, and by so doing, evade a manhunt that had involved some 13,000 police officers.[35] The exploit appeared to have been so precisely executed, and the police efforts so fruitless that it was suspected that foreign intelligence agents had been involved. The fact that Moro had been engaged in negotiations to bring Communist support for the DC government of Giulio Andreotti heightened these suspicions.[36] But despite these initial reactions, after both judicial and parliamentary investigations, those eventually arrested, tried and convicted in connection with the Moro case were found to be Italians, members of the BR's Roman Column.[37] The latter had been organized by Mario Morretti, one of the few members of the group's "historic nucleus" to have avoided arrest by 1975.

The 55 days during which Moro was held captive were one of profound crisis for the Italian political system. The BR issued demands for Moro's release: Moro in exchange for the release of their own "political prisoners", the "historic nucleus" and other jailed members of the organization. Neither the government nor the DC and PCI leaderships were willing to strike such a bargain. The Socialist party under the direction of its new secretary, Bettino Craxi, was more receptive. For his part, Moro was permitted by his captors to send letters to his colleagues in government and the DC leadership in which he pleaded for his life, requesting that they negotiate an exchange with the BR. Moro cited other instances in which governments had yielded to terrorist demands in exchange for the lives of kidnap victims.[38] But neither Moro's letters to his colleagues nor appeals to the BR from the Pope and the secretary general of the United Nations prevailed.

Our principal concern with the Moro kidnapping and assassination is with its impact on revolutionary terrorism in Italy. The BR had achieved a "military" success in its campaign against the Italian state. But was the venture also a political victory? The answer is that it obviously was not.

Insofar as the BR is concerned, the Moro killing initiated a process of dissidence and fragmentation within the organization. Valerio Morucci and Adriana Faranda, two members of the Roman column who had expressed their opposition to killing Moro during the period of his captivity, left the BR after the murder, taking with them other militants sympathetic to their point of view. Morucci and Faranda, along with the other dissidents, formed their own band, the Popular Movement for Offensive Resistance, and proclaimed that the cause of revolution had been harmed by the Moro tragedy.[39]

Later the BR organization in Milan, the Walter Alasia Column, also broke with the central direction.[40] The Milanese accused the BR leadership of "having completely failed, of being by now totally outside the place of work, of having lost any link with the working class."[41] Members of the group claimed it was only they, the Walter Alasia Column, that maintained any serious ties with the proletariat. Similar sentiments about the BR's national direction were expressed from their prison cells by Curcio and other members of the "historic nucleus"; in fact, they had encouraged the Milanese dissidents.

Not only did the Moro killing stimulate a process of disintegration within the BR, but it also served to sour its relations with other revolutionary groups active in Italy. The BR's Strategic Direction had hoped that the Moro episode would actually serve to unify all the terrorist organizations. Instead, it had the effect of worsening their relations. Leaders of Front Line later testified that prior to the kidnappings they had not had any contacts with the BR or been aware of its intentions concerning Moro. And when the PL leaders were approached by the BR and asked for assistance during the kidnapping, they declined to provide it. Likewise, some leaders of AO viewed the Moro case as a major mistake, an act, as they saw it, that invited state repression of all revolutionary groups. Yet other AO leaders saw positive things in the killing; the Moro kidnapping showed the weakness of the state and revealed the BR's efficiency.

At least one group of observers considered the event to have been an unqualified success. Representatives of the PLO, George Habbash's Popular Front for the Liberation of Palestine in particular, regarded it as proof that the BR ought to be taken seriously. After Moro's death, discussions were held in Paris between Moretti from the BR and PLO representatives. The latter agreed to provide the BR with substantial quantities of arms if the organization agreed to attack Israeli and NATO targets located in Italy.[42]

The spiral of murder, kidnapping and assault did not descend in the aftermath of Moro's death. Magistrates, politicians, trade unionists and a wide assortment of other representatives of the bourgeois system continued to be targets for attack over the next several years. In the case of both the BR and PL, there was a very discernible increase in their assaults on police officers, those belonging to special anti-terrorist detachments especially.

These attacks on the police were made for good reason from the terrorists' point of view. They were reactions to the fact that the authorities began to enjoy considerable success in detecting and arresting the terrorists. Because of changes in the law, the authorities were able to offer those they apprehended immunity or a reduction in sentence if they became "repentants", that is if they disassociated themselves from their terrorist organization and were willing to identify other members of their bands. After experiencing several years of life in clandestinity, many of those arrested were willing to repent in exchange for the possibility of a return to normal life.[43] The result was that the police were able to gather a harvest of hundreds of terrorists in 1980. And even when they succeeded in evading arrest for the moment, the authorities were able to identify such important figures in the BR and PL as Enrico Fenzi, a professor of literature at the University of Genoa and head of the BR column in that city; Giovanni Senzani, a professor of sociology at the University of Florence and head of the BR's Naples column; and Marco Donat Cattin, a PL leader and son of the Christian Democratic cabinet member. Further, in April 1979 AO was decapitated when Antonio Negri and other academics at the University of Padua were arrested.

Front Line began to experience the same symptoms of decay as the BR. In 1979 PL dissidents concluded that there was little point in continuing the armed struggle as it was currently being practiced. They separated themselves from the organization and created their own band, For Communism. In Milan during the following year, still other PL dissidents established Organized Communists for Proletarian Liberation (COLP).[44]

Measured in terms of the deaths and injuries inflicted by the revolutionary groups, the years 1978, 1979 and 1980 were clearly the high points. In these three years a total of 206 people were either killed or seriously injured as the result of attacks by the BR, PL or the smaller formations.[45] If we take the two succeeding years together, 1981-82, the figure declines to a total of 66 deaths or serious injuries, a number almost identical to that reached (65) in the 1976-77 period. Furthermore, there is also a very noticeable shift in targets. During the three peak years, the revolutionaries' most common victims were businessmen, politicians and professional people (journalists, lawyers, teachers). For 1981-82, on the other hand, in the context of an overall decline in the frequency of attacks, there is a dramatic increase in the proportion of terrorist assaults directed against the police, defecting members of their own organizations, as well as on the families of repentant terrorists. In 1982 more than three quarters of the recorded attacks were aimed at such targets.[46]

The explanation for these developments is not hard to come by. The revolutionaries were by now clearly on the defensive, with hundreds of them being arrested during 1981-82. The shifting pattern of attack was a reaction to the successes of the authorities committed to the eradication of terrorism, and had more to do with the terrorist groups' defensive needs and personal vendettas than with the program of revolutionary violence on which they had embarked.

On December 18, 1981 the BR, or more precisely, its column in the Veneto, made an effort to retrieve this rapidly deteriorating situation. On that date a BR unit under the direction of Antonio Savasta kidnapped the American General and NATO officer, James Dozier from his home in Verona.[47]

The Dozier kidnapping represents a case where the evidence clearly suggests the existence of communication between the BR and a foreign intelligence agency, the Bulgarian to be precise.[48] In their contacts with other European terrorist groups and the PLO, the BR had acquired the reputation of being "provincials." The organization's primary interest had been with making a revolution in Italy. The BR leadership had been determined not to become the pawns of forces from outside the country. Furthermore, BR doctrine had defined the Soviet Union in uncomplimentary terms as "social imperialist," a designation hardly designed to win applause from Warsaw Pact regimes. But in the Dozier case, the BR sought the help of two intermediaries, Luigi and Loris Scricciolo, the former a trade union official, in order to establish contact with the Bulgarians. The BR hoped that, in exchange for the NATO secrets that might be extracted from General Dozier, the Bulgarians would provide weapons and money so that the revolutionary struggle could be continued.

But obtaining NATO secrets from Dozier proved difficult. Not only was he a person of considerable courage, but he did not speak Italian. And astonishingly, this fact was not anticipated by his captors because, as it turned out, none of them were capable of speaking English.[49] In view of this situation, the amount of information available for sale to the Bulgarians was not substantial. For their part, the Bulgarians turned out to be far more wary of becoming involved in dealing with the BR than the latter had anticipated, or should have anticipated, since suspicions about the Bulgarians had been raised already in connection with the assassination attempt on the Pope.

General Dozier was liberated on January 28, 1982 by a special anti-terrorist contingent of the state police. Acting on information given them by a newly repentant BR member in their custody, the police broke into an apartment in Padua, freed Dozier and arrested his five captors, including Savasta.

The operation proved to be an enormous disaster for the BR as well as the other revolutionary groups. By the middle of April, the police reported having arrested 225 terrorists since the first of the year.[50] As in the Moro case, the Dozier kidnapping had given the BR part of what it wanted: massive publicity. But the attention led the police to arrest as many BR members as they could find. These arrests produced more "repentants", including Savasta, and more "repentants" yielded still more arrests.

Thus, by the end of 1982, many, though not all, of the revolutionary terrorists had been captured. Some managed to evade the net and flee into exile in France. Not all those arrested decided to abandon their revolutionary principles and comrades, some called for a continuation of the struggle. Collections of their various prescriptions to this end, written in prison, were published in 1983.[51]

It is a testimony to its ability to endure and attract new recruits that the Red Brigades was able to assassinate the American diplomat Leamon Hunt in Rome in February 1984. Hunt's murder, along with the Dozier kidnapping, suggested that those BR members still at large had abandoned the organization's "provincialism." These acts had little to do with making a revolution in Italy and more with international concerns with NATO and on behalf of interests largely extraneous to political developments in their own country. Hunt's murder also served as a warning, one echoed by Italy's leading state investigators, that terrorism, though defeated, had not come to a complete end in the country.[52]

Failure

Viewing it in retrospect, what should we conclude about the recent experience of revolutionary terrorism in Italy? After writing the 1,300 page *sentenza* against the Florentine members of Front Line, Judge Marcello De Roberto concluded that the defeat of terrorism represented a triumph for the Italian people.[53] He reasoned that never in these years had the terrorist groups been able to acquire a mass following that could have transformed them into a serious menace to the democratic order. The good sense of the people had made the victory of the revolutionaries impossible. Writing from a very different perspective, Patrizio Peci, the "repentant" BR leader, also linked the defeat of revolutionary terrorism to the character of the Italian people. However, while De Roberto pointed to their good judgment, Peci referred bitterly to their deficiencies, as he understood them. "Italy will never become a truly Communist country, not only because of the Church, NATO, the industrial powers, etc., but above all because of the way Italians are made, they are individualists and don't love Communism. . . . Almost always a country gets the government it deserves."[54]

It is possible to explain the collapse of the terrorist enterprise without reference either to the good sense or individualism of the Italian people, most of whom watched the events described in this chapter on television or read about them in their newspapers. Instead, the failure of the revolutionaries may well have been the result of the methods they chose. The choice of clandestine violence served to isolate the revolutionaries from those segments of society in whose name they sought to make a revolution, a judgment about the terrorist method that Marx, Lenin and Trotsky, the authors of the terrorists' sacred texts, had reached many years earlier. Yet it is also clear that the terrorist groups managed to strike a responsive chord among some Italians that revolutionary terrorist bands active in other western democracies never managed to reach.

In these democracies, ideologically motivated terrorists succeeded in attracting hundreds of members and followers. In Italy, the comparable figures numbered in the thousands. Where did these people come from? What led them to join the terrorist organizations? These crucial questions are ones which will be addressed in the next chapter.

Notes

1. Giovanni Bechelloni, *Cultura e ideologia nella nuova sinistra* (Milan: Comunita, 1973) p. XII.

2. Quoted in Giuseppe Vettori (ed.), *La sinistra extraparlamentare in Italia* (Rome: Newton Compton, 1973) p. 307.

3. Soccorso Rosso (eds.), *Brigate Rosse* (Milan: Feltrinelli, 1976) p. 34.

4. Luigi Bobbio, *Lotta Continua* (Rome: Savelli, 1979) pp. 5–21.

5. Giampaolo Pansa, *Storie italiane di violenza e terrorismo* (Bari: Laterza, 1980) pp. 10–12.

6. Mino Monicelli, *La follia veneta* (Rome: Riuniti, 1981) pp. 68–75.

7. Thomas Sheehan, "Italy: Behind the Ski Mask," *The New York Review of Books* 26:13 (August, 1979) p. 21.

8. Mino Monicelli, *L'Ultrasinistra in Italia*: 1968–1978 (Bari: Laterza, 1978) pp. 44–47.

9. Fini and Barberi, *op. cit.*, pp. 20–21.

10. *La Stampa* (May 18, 1973) p. 1.

11. Committee on The Judiciary United States Senate, Report of the Subcommittee on Security and Terrorism, *Terrorism and Security: The Italian Experience* (Washington, D.C.: U.S. Government Printing Office, 1984) pp. 39–40.

12. *La Stampa* (September 18, 1971) p. 20.

13. Mario Sossi, *Nella prigione delle BR* (Milan: Editoriale Nuova, 1979) pp. 79–81.

14. Corte D'Assise D'Appello Di Milano, *Sentenza* N. 7/80 (April 1–9, 1981) pp. 28–29.

15. *Ibid.*, pp. 51–52. See also Giudice Istruttore Francesco Amato, *Ordinanza/ Sentenza* N. 10607/69 Tribunale di Roma, pp. 771–776.

16. Vincenzo Tessandori, *BR: Imputazione banda armata* (Milan: Garzanti, 1977) pp. 28–58; Soccorso Rosso (eds.), *op. cit.*, pp. 26–85; Alessandro Silj, *Never Again Without a Rifle* (New York: Karz Publishers, 1979) pp. 3–116.

17. Gian Carlo Caselli and Donatella della Porta, "per una storia del terrorismo di sinistra," (A report delivered at the Istituto Cattaneo conference on political violence and terrorism in Italy, Bologna, April 29–30, 1983) pp. 6–7.

18. Corte D'Assise Di Roma, *Sentenza* 31/81RG (January 24, 1983) p. 661.

19. *Ibid.*, p. 662.

20. Sossi, *op. cit.*, p. 16.

21. On the origins of NAP see Soccorso Rosso Napoletano (eds.), *I NAP: Storia dei nuclei armati proletari* (Milan: Colletivo editoriale Libri Rossi, 1976) pp. 129–133; silj, *op. cit.*, pp. 119–157.

22. *La Stampa* (March 20, 1975) p. 2.

23. *La Repubblica* (December 15, 1976) p. 1.

24. La Repubblica (December 18, 1976) p. 3.

25. Emilio Papa, *Il processo alle Brigate Rosse* (Turin: Giappichelli, 1979) pp. 20–52.

26. Corte Di Assise Di Roma *Sentenza* 31/81RG, *op. cit.*, p. 703; see also Angelo Ventura, "Il problema delle origine del terrorismo di sinistra," in Donatella della Porta (ed.), *Terrorismi in Italia* (Bologna: Il Mulino, 1984) pp. 133–142.

27. Corte D'Assise di Torino, *Sentenza* N. 17/81 (July 28, 1981) pp. 111–112; Corte diFirenze, *Sentenza* (April 4, 1983) pp. 135–136.

28. Luciana Stortoni, Analisi di una organizzazione terrorista: Prima Linea (tesi di laurea, Political Science Faculty, Universitiy of Florence, 1983) pp. 141–152.

29. La Repubblica (February 19, 1977) p. 1.

30. Fabio Mussi, *Bologna '77* (Rome Riuniti, 1978) pp. 23–26.

31. Francesco Amato, Giudice Istruttore, *Ordinanza/Sentenza* N 1027/79, Tribunale di Roma, *op. cit.*, pp. 228–250; see also, Lucio Castellano (ed.), *Aut Op: la storia e i documenti da potere operaio all'autonomia organizzata* (Milan: Savelli, 1980) ad passim.

32. Carlo Rossella, "Sapore di golpe," *Panorama* 25:573 (April, 1977) pp. 42–44.

33. Senato della Repubblica - Camera dei Deputati, *Relazione della commissione parlamentare sulla strage di via fani, sul sequestro e l'assasino di Aldo Moro e sul terrorismo in Italia* (Rome: Tipografia del Senato, 1983) p. 13.

34. Pansa, *Storia italiane di violenza e terrorismo, op. cit.*, pp. 103–111.

35. *Relazione, op. cit.*, p. 36.

36. Nazareno Pagani and Matteo Spina, "Quel giovedi di paura," *Panorama* 26:623 (March, 1978) pp. 38–43.

37. Corte d'Assise di Roma, *Sentenza 2/83, op. cit.*, pp. 1–20.

38. Moro's letters are reproduced in the minority reports of the parliamentary investigating committee, *Relazione op. cit.*, pp. 91–123.

39. *Relazione* of majority, *op. cit.*, pp. 115–119.

40. The Walter Alasia column took its name from a young BR killed by the police in 1976, see Giorgio Manzini, *Indagine su un brigatista rosso* (Turin: Einaudi, 1978).

41. Quoted in, Giudice Istruttore, Tribunale Civile e Penale di Milano, *Sentenza/Ordinanza* N. 490/81F (May 15, 1983) p. 118.

42. Majority *Relazione, op. cit.*, pp. 132–133.

43. Giodano Bruno Guerri (ed.), *Patrizio Peci: io l'infame* (Milan: Mondaddori, 1983).

44. Giudice Istruttore, Tribunale Civile e Penale di Minalo, *Sentenza/Ordinanza* 23/82, p. 109.

45. Donatella della Porta and Maurizio Rossi, *I terrorismi in Italia tra il 1969 e il 1982* (Bologna: Catteneo, 1983) p. 7.

46. *Ibid.*, p. 19.

47. *La Stampa* (December 19, 1981) p. 1.

48. Majority *Relazione op. cit.*, pp. 148–151.

49. Interview with Frederic Vreeland, political counselor at the U.S. Embassy in Rome during this period (interview June 18, 1984, Rome).

50. *La Stampa* (April 16, 1982) p. 1.

51. Andrea Coi, Prospero Gallinari, Francesco Piccioni and Bruno Seghetti, *Politica e rivoluzione* (Milan: Giuseppe Mai, 1983); Andrea Coi, *Italia 1983: prigionieri, processi, progett* (Rome: Cooperativa Apache, 1983).

52. *La Repubblica* (June 2, 1984) p. 14.

53. Interview with writer, Florence, April 6, 1984.

54. Guerri (ed.), *op. cit.*, p. 220.

5
WHO WERE
THE TERRORISTS?

There is no lack of biography and even autobiography of modern terrorists. The student of the subject or the casual reader has a wide assortment of these accounts from which to choose. The lives of such figures as the international terrorist Vladimir Illich Sanchez (Carlos the Jackal), Ulrike Meinhof and her cohorts from the German Red Army Faction, as well as any number of others have been discussed in the kind of detail usually reserved for important political leaders.[1] The same applies in the Italian case. Giangiacomo Feltrinelli, Renato Curcio, Margherita Cagol, Patrizio Peci and a handful of others have had their lives described in books and periodicals.[2]

But how representative are the subjects of these biographies of terrorists in general? In the case of a small band, such as the Symbionese Liberation Army in the United States, telling the story of three of four members may be sufficient to understand what led the group to behave as it did because the band itself did not consist of more than a handful of adherents. In the Italian case, however, such a procedure will not work. As in the case of a journalist attempting to extrapolate the sentiments of the American electorate by interviewing passersby at an airport, discerning the backgrounds of Italian terrorists from Feltrinelli, Curcio et. al., is inappropriate. There were several thousand Italians who planned, aided or committed acts of political terrorism during the 1970s and 80s.

To be sure, observers of political terrorism have sought to go beyond the realm of the single biography to that of a sociology of terrorism. Efforts have been undertaken to understand the social composition of terrorist groups active in different nations and to develop cross-national profiles of terrorists in general.

Reactions to these efforts have been mixed. After reviewing some of the evidence, one historian concluded that terrorists appear to have been drawn from all sorts of family backgrounds and social milieu.[3] If this is true, then no generalizations would be possible.

At the other extreme, there have been any number of psychiatrists and other psychologically informed observers who have been willing to make global generalizations about the terrorist personality and the particular family circumstances in which it will be formed. Instead of concluding that terrorists may come from anywhere, or nowhere, these observers have been willing to be precise in specifying the conditions that will stimulate individuals to become terrorists. The problem with this approach is that the observers tend to generalize freely based on a combination of prevailing theories of abnormal psychology and a handful of case histories used for purposes of illustrating these theories.

Located somewhere in the middle of these discussions is the body of evidence concerning who the modern terrorists are and where they came from. To the extent that a group portrait emerges from this evidence, it looks, approximately, like this. Terrorists tend to come from the higher strata of society, not from its deprived. Often they are young and frequently they are former university students who have become frustrated by too much talk and not enough action about revolution, or by their attempts to apply abstract theories of mass revolution to situations which turn out to be incompatible with the theories. Most terrorists are men, but at least in some countries, women have not been completely immune to the allure of terrorism. Although there have been some well publicized exceptions, women have tended to play subordinate roles in terrorist organizations, ones involving the provision of logistical support to their male counterparts. Finally, terrorists tend to be city dwellers, who were either born in or were long time residents of the communities in which their acts of violence were committed.[4]

If this is the overall picture, to what extent does it capture the background of Italian terrorists? There are several reasons why the Italian experience provides us with an excellent opportunity to understand what sorts of people become terrorists. For one, there is the sheer volume of people who got caught up in the violence. Secondly, because the country's experience went on for so long, an examination of who the terrorists were can add a temporal element to the analysis. Were the types of people who became involved in terrorism at the beginning of the 1970s the same sorts of individuals who were attracted to it in 1977 and later, after the first wave of terrorist organizations had collapsed? Thirdly, since Italy experienced both left-wing revolutionary and neo-Fascist terrorism, there is the obvious question of whether or not there were any meaningful differences between people who committed the violence in the name of proletarian revolution and those who did so in support of the neo-Fascist doctrines discussed earlier. Does Left and Right make a difference when it comes to the backgrounds of terrorists?

In order to address these questions, biographical information was acquired about individuals who were arrested (or for whom warrants were issued) for having planned, assisted or committed acts of political terrorism in Italy between 1970 and 1984. Information was obtained from two newspapers, La Stampa (Turin) and La Repubblica (Rome), as well as the court records (requisitorie, ordinanze/sentenze and sentenze) from some, but not all, of the major terrorist trials.[5] The result of this endeavor was an accumulation of biographical information about 2,512 individuals who met the above description. The collection is not based on a sample, but instead represents a reasonably complete listing of persons identified as having engaged in terrorism over this 15 year period.

The Overall Pattern

Who were these people? Where did they come from? The data recorded in Table 5.1 show the terrorists' general biographical characteristics, irrespective of whether they were leftists or neo-Fascists or when in the development of Italian terrorism they were arrested or identified.

As these data reveal, the portrait is of a group of predominantly young people, the majority of whom were in their 20s at the time of their detection by the authorities. And although a little under a fifth of the terrorists were women, we are still dealing with a largely male population.

In terms of central tendency, pluralities of the terrorists were born in industrialized northern Italy and in big cities as well. Nonetheless, there is a substantial representation of individuals from the South and from smaller communities. If we compare the terrorists' places of legal residence with the communities in which they were born, it is clear that they were a rather mobile group. The general pattern is that of movement from small communities, medium-sized cities and the South (including Sicily and Sardinia) to the North and the major cities at some point in their lives. There is then some truth in the views of the recent mayors of Bologna and Turin who explained terrorism in their cities by reference to the arrival of newcomers, especially from the South, to their communities.[6] And, in view of the terrorists' average age, it also appears that many of them were recent migrants to the big cities.

A review of their occupational backgrounds suggests that the terrorists were drawn from most strata of Italian society, with the exception of the agricultural sector. Industrialists, business managers and aristocrats are to be found along with professional criminals, prostitutes and other "subproletarians". Yet despite the wide array of backgrounds, their representation was far from uniform; some segments of Italian society made more substantial

TABLE 5.1
Profile of Italian Terrorists, 1970-1984

Biographical Characteristic	Number (Per Cent)	
Sex		
Male	2061	(82.0)
Female	451	(18.0)
Total	2512	(100.0)
Age at Time of Arrest/Identification		
15 to 19	197	(9.0)
20 to 24	825	(36.0)
25 to 29	666	(29.0)
30 to 34	346	(15.0)
35 to 39	132	(6.0)
40 to 44	61	(3.0)
45 to 49	33	(1.0)
50 and over	48	(2.0)
Total	2308	(100.0)
Place of Birth (Region)		
North	577	(43.0)
Center	161	(12.0)
Rome	234	(17.0)
South	333	(25.0)
Foreign Born	42	(3.0)
Total	1347	(100.0)
Place of Birth (Size of Community)		
Small Community (under 100,000 population)	449	(30.0)
Medium-sized City (100,000 to one million population)	445	(30.0)
Big City (over one million population)	552	(37.0)
Foreign Born	42	(3.0)
Total	1347	(100.0)
Place of Legal Residence (Region)		
North	1299	(53.0)
Center	252	(10.0)
Rome	594	(24.0)
South	293	(12.0)
Foreign Born	3	(0.0)
Total	2441	(100.0)

TABLE 5.1 (continued)
Profile of Italian Terrorists, 1970–1984

Biographical Characteristics	Number	(Per Cent)
Place of Legal Residence (size of community)		
Small Community (under 100,000 population)	251	(10.0)
Medium sized City (100,000 to one million population)	592	(24.0)
Big City (over one million population)	1606	(65.0)
Foreign	3	(0.0)
Total	2452	(100.0)
Related by Family to Other Terrorist		
Yes	320	(13.0)
No	2185	(87.0)
Total	2505	(100.0)
Type of Family Relationship		
Marital	139	(43.0)
Sibling	151	(47.0)
Parental	12	(4.0)
Other	18	(6.0)
Total	320	(100.0)
Occupation		
Criminal, subproletarian	69	(5.0)
Student	382	(27.0)
Manual Worker	365	(26.0)
Police, Military,Bodyguard	54	(4.0)
White Collar Clerk	220	(15.0)
Small Business (salesman, shopkeeper, artisan)	60	(4.0)
Free Professional (lawyer,architect,journalist,physician,business manager, industrialist)	100	(7.0)
Aristocrat	41	(3.0)
Housewife	11	(1.0)
Total	1430	(100.0)
Previous Political Party Membership		
Left (Communist and Socialist)	66	(23.0)
Center (Christian Democrats and Others)	4	(1.0)
Right (Italian Social Movement)	216	(76.0)
Total	286	(100.0)

TABLE 5.1
Profile of Italian Terrorists, 1970–1984 (continued)

Biographical Characteristics	Number	(Per Cent)
Previous Membership in Extraparliamentary Groups		
Left	388	(60.0)
Right	264	(40.0)
Total	652	(100.0)

contributions to the terrorist population than others. The largest categories reported in the table are students, manual workers, white collar employees and teachers (including university professors). Based on what is known about terrorists, from both the cross-national studies and the account of Italian terrorism in the previous chapter, the presence of a large number of students does not come as a great shock. Neither, for that matter, should it come as a surprise to discover the relatively high percentage of teachers and free professionals found among the terrorists. Intellectuals, after all, are scarcely unknown elements in terrorist organizations. On the other hand, the large number of manual workers, more than a quarter of the total, attracted to these organizations does seem exceptionally high compared to expectations derived from the cross-national studies. The same may be said in connection with the large number of white collar employees in the population. The overall impression with which we are left is that the Italian terrorist organizations were able to penetrate far deeper into the country's social structure than has been the case with terrorist groups active in other Western democracies.

The data also make it possible for us to explore some of the personal and political experiences these individuals had before they became involved in terrorism. Although the information available is very incomplete, it appears that many of the terrorists had previous affiliations with conventional political parties. These affiliations were almost all with parties at the Left and Right ends of the spectrum. There were very few people who drifted into terrorism after membership in parties at the Center in the Italian system. Further, a not inconsiderable proportion of the terrorist population was composed of former members of both the left-wing and rightist extraparliamentary movements. Thus, to the extent that the terrorists had earlier exposures to political life; these were experiences that placed them at the ideological poles of the system.

Over the years, observers of Italian society have emphasized the importance of the family. In this light, the family appears to have played a role in the decision to become a terrorist. Thirteen per cent of the individuals in the terrorist population were related to one another, most commonly as husbands and wives. If we were to speculate that the population likely included an unknown number of unmarried couples, along with siblings, it seems reasonable to suspect that the decision to become a terrorist was often not that of individual choice. Likely it involved a decision, and a gradual one at that, by a primary group whose members reached consensus over the desirability of violent political engagement.

Compared to the general profile of terrorists derived from cross-national studies, the Italian ones seem different in at least two ways. First, the Italians were more likely to have been born in smaller communities and to have been recent migrants to the major metropolitan areas than the global picture would suggest. Second, the Italians' occupational backgrounds reflect a higher representation of working class people than might have been expected.

The Revolutionaries and Neo-Fascists Compared

The above commentary described some of the important characteristics of Italian terrorists in general. It did not distinguish among them based on the kinds of violent organizations with which they chose to become affiliated. But does group affiliation make any difference? Morally terrorists are terrorists no matter if they commit violent acts on behalf of neo-Fascist or leftist revolutionary groups. But are the same kind of people attracted to right and left-wing terrorist organizations? Certainly studies of voting behavior and political parties in Italy and elsewhere have discovered the existence of meaningful differences in the backgrounds of those who vote for and belong to right and left-wing political parties. Terrorist groups are, after all, political organizations. Does not it follow that their members would also exhibit similar differences?

The evidence (see Table 5.2) is striking and compels the conclusion that the neo-Fascist and leftist revolutionary terrorists in Italy were very different groups of people. The left-wing organizations were able to attract a substantial number of women (23 per cent of the total), while the neo-Fascist groups were composed overwhelmingly of men. The ages of the two groups were also significantly different. Here the neo-Fascists succeeded in attracting higher proportions of individuals at both ends of the age distribution, under 20 and over 40, than did the leftists. (Gamma = .22)

Members of the two groups tended to come from different parts of Italy. The leftists' backgrounds were more geographically diverse. As against the neo-Fascists, they were more likely to have been born in smaller communities and medium-sized cities, as well as outside the country. Further, they drew

TABLE 5.2
Differences Between Left-Wing and Neo-Fascist Terrorists in Italy

Place of Residence (Region)

Group	North	Center	Rome	South	Foreign Born	Total
Left	1014	178	282	231	1	1706
	(59.4)	(10.4)	(16.5)	(13.5)	(0.1)	(75.3)
Right	194	52	290	22	2	560
	(34.6)	(9.3)	(51.8)	(3.9)	(0.4)	(24.7)
Total	1208	230	572	253	3	2266

$\chi^2 = 294.50$ $p < .001$ df = 4

Place of Residence (Size of Community)

Group	Small Community	Medium City	Big City	Total
Left	199	389	1125	1713
	(11.6)	(22.7)	(65.6)	(75.3)
Right	41	133	386	562
	(7.3)	(23.7)	(68.7)	(24.7)
Total	240	522	1511	2276

$\chi^2 = 11.08$ $p < .01$ df = 2

Nature of Family Relations

Group	Marital	Sibling	Parental	Other	Total
Left	127	109	6	13	255
	(49.8)	(42.7)	(2.4)	(5.0)	(83.6)
Right	9	30	6	5	50
	(18.0)	(60.0)	(12.0)	(10.0)	(16.4)
Total	136	139	12	18	305

$\chi^2 = 12.80$ $p < .001$ df = 3

TABLE 5.2 (continued)
Differences Between Left-Wing and Neo-Fascist Terrorists in Italy

Sex

Group	Male	Female	Total
Left	1357 (77.0)*	406 (23.0)	1763 (75.5)
Right	533 (93.2)	39 (6.8)	572 (24.5)
Total	1890	445	2335

$\chi^2 = 72.52$ $p < .001$ df = 1

Place of Birth (Region)

Group	North	Center	Rome	South	Foreign Born	Total
Left	380 (49.9)	110 (13.0)	66 (7.6)	257 (30.4)	33 (3.9)	846 (69.1)
Right	124 (32.8)	37 (9.8)	155 (41.0)	53 (14.0)	9 (2.4)	378 (30.9)
Total	504	147	221	310	42	1224

$\chi^2 = 200.45$ $p < .001$ df = 4

Place of Birth (Size of Community)

Group	Small Community	Medium City	Big City	Foreign Born	Total
Left	373 (38.5)	274 (28.2)	290 (29.9)	33 (3.4)	970 (71.1)
Right	67 (17.0)	122 (28.4)	206 (52.3)	9 (2.3)	394 (28.9)
Total	440	386	496	42	1364

$\chi^2 = 79.72$ $p < .001$ df = 3

TABLE 5.2 (continued)
Differences Between Left-Wing and Neo-Fascist Terrorists in Italy

Prior Political Party Affiliation**

Group	Left	Center	Right	Total
Left	62 (91.2)	2 (2.9)	4 (5.9)	68 (44.4)
Right	1 (1.2)	2 (2.9)	82 (96.5)	85 (55.6)
Total	63	4	86	153

χ^2 = 129.52   p < .001   df = 2

Occupational Differences

Group	Criminal, Subproletarian	Worker	Student	Military Police	White Collar Impiegato	Small Business
Left	58 (5.2)	355 (29.8)	301 (26.8)	14 (1.2)	198 (17.6)	29 (2.6)
Right	5 (2.1)	20 (8.4)	50 (21.1)	37 (15.6)	20 (8.4)	29 (12.2)
Total	63	375	351	51	218	58

Group	Teacher	Free Professional	Industrialist/ Business Manager/ Aristocrat	Housewife	Total
Left	110 (9.8)	61 (5.4)	8 (0.7)	11 (1.0)	1125 (82.6)
Right	14 (5.9)	35 (14.8)	27 (11.4)	0 (0.0)	237 (17.4)
Total	124	96	35	11	1362

χ^2 = 318.33   p < .001   df = 9

---

*Percentages in parentheses are row percentages; those in Total column are overall percentages.

**The Left parties were the Communists and Socialists. Parties of the Right were the MSI and Monarchists. The Christian Democrats along with the Liberals and Republicans were considered the Center.

higher proportions of their adherents from the northern and southern regions. By contrast the neo-Fascists were more rooted in the big cities and Rome especially.

When we compare their places of birth with the localities of their adult residence, the leftists appear to have been a far more mobile group; the neo-Fascists were more likely to have remained in the communities in which they were born. The leftists tended to have migrated from smaller communities and medium-sized cities to the major metropolitan areas (Rome, Milan, Turin) and from the South to the North before developing their links to terrorist organizations.

Occupational background also serves to distinguish left from right. Studies of this characteristic in other countries have suggested this generalization. Leftist terrorists tend to be drawn from the upper strata of society. They are often the sons and daughters of the establishment. Right-wing terrorists in France and West Germany, on the other hand, often come from lower class circumstances.[7] In these countries right-wing terrorism seems to have been inspired by ethnic and racial resentments directed against "guest workers" and other immigrants, elements largely missing from the Italian scene. Whatever the sources of its inspiration, these observations leave us with a peculiar inversion of the occupational or class backgrounds of left and right-wing political parties: where we would expect the former to derive its support from the lower strata and the latter from the upper, terrorist organizations appear upside down in terms of their class composition.

This is not the case in Italy, however. As the data recorded in Table 5.2 reveal, the neo-Fascists were over-represented among individuals with lower-middle class backgrounds in small business (salesmen, shopkeepers, artisans), among career military officers and policemen, along with free professionals, industrialists, business managers and those of aristocratic origins. Aside from the significant contingent of students, the occupational distribution reflected in the neo-Fascists' backgrounds looks approximately like one might expect to find with a conservative or right-wing political party in an industrialized society.

Individuals with high status occupations are not missing from the leftists' ranks either; there is certainly a substantial contingent from the free professions (law, medicine, journalism, architecture). But as the overall distribution of occupations makes obvious, the left-wing groups were successful in recruiting a high proportion of their members from precisely those segments of the population in whose name they sought to make a revolution. If the occupational distribution of the neo-Fascists is skewed towards the upper strata, that of the leftists is skewed towards the lower. Manual workers, subproletarians and white collar clerks are all significantly over-represented. And, as with the memberships of left-wing political parties in Western Europe, teachers makeup a meaningful proportion of the revolutionary terrorists.

On reflection, these results should not come as a surprise. Given the intensity of their ideological and organizational commitments to the Italian working class and to marginal segments of the population (e.g., prison inmates), the fact that the revolutionary groups were able to derive some of their membership from individuals with these backgrounds should not seem astonishing.

The comparatively successful appeal of the revolutionary groups to persons with working class and subproletarian backgrounds was likely the result of several additional factors. For one, despite the fact that the PCI and the major PCI dominated trade union the General Confederation of Italian Workers (CGIL) had abandoned their revolutionary tactics a long time ago, the same cannot be said about their doctrinal pronouncements. They continued to contain approving references to Marx, Lenin and various luminaries of the Third International. This gap between Marxist-Leninist rhetoric and reformist reality may have left at least some workers with the impression that the triumph of the proletariat by means of violent revolution was a goal that ought to be pursued, if not by the inoffensive figures controlling the PCI, then by those movements and terrorist groups which claimed to be converting the historically and culturally approved rhetoric into something approximating reality.

In this regard, it is worth noting that of the 335 manual workers who belonged to the leftist terrorist groups, 67 (20 per cent) were reported to have been members of labor unions. Furthermore, there were 46 left-wing terrorists (13 percent of the workers, but 68 per cent of the union members) who had played leadership roles at the plant level in either union organizations or factory councils. These figures lend themselves to a variety of interpretations. At a minimum, it seems fair to say that union membership and even leadership did not represent an insuperable barrier to recruitment into the terrorist organizations. There was apparently little that was incompatible between exposure to and advocacy of PCI and CGIL rhetoric and terrorist involvement. Yet the case should not be overstated. Obviously the vast majority of unionized workers did not become revolutionary terrorists.

A second factor which may have contributed to the working class presence in the terrorist groups is the extraparliamentary political movements. As we have observed, these revolutionary movements, active in Milan, Turin and other highly industrialized communities, were organizations which attracted both radicalized students and workers. The movements, in turn, constituted a pool from which the terrorist groups drew a fair number of their adherents. It is likely that it was from among these already radicalized workers that many of the working class terrorists came.

Finally, the fact that left-wing terrorism persisted in Italy for a comparatively long period may have contributed to the large worker representation. In situations where revolutionary terrorism is quickly repressed by the authorities, the terrorists taken into custody are likely to be the founders of the group or the initiators of the violence. Correlatively, this core of individuals is likely to be made up of the largely middle class intellectuals who form the basis of revolutionary movements in general. In Italy, the persistence of leftist terrorism may have permitted the groups enough time to create organizational networks in plants and factories where their cadres could recruit members among their targeted clientele. This is an issue to which we will return.

The occupational backgrounds of the neo-fascists also requires some interpretation. The affinity of so many industrialists, business managers and police/military officers for the neo-Fascist organizations is, in part, the product of the means by which these groups sought to seize power in the first half of the 1970s. A strategy designed to promote a coup d'état, as against a mass revolution, almost by definition required the involvement of people possessing substantial political and financial resources, as well as access to the levers of power in the existing political order. The members of any group seeking to achieve power by means of a coup would take on many of the biographical characteristics of the Italian neo-Fascists.

But this line of reasoning only takes the interpretation back one step. It also begs the question of why some elements in the business community were attracted to the anti-democratic schemes of the neo-Fascist groups. An answer that makes some sense is that many of these individuals, particularly the older ones in the *Fronte Nazionale* and the *Rosa dei Venti*, had never reconciled themselves to Italian democracy. More generally, however, they and their younger cohorts were reacting to the partially fantastic dangers of Red revolution. Certainly the violent neo-Fascists tended to be drawn from those segments of the population who had every reason to feel threatened by the revolutionary appeals of the extraparliamentary movements, as well as by the PCI's seemingly irreversible march towards power in the 70s.

In thinking about the occupational backgrounds of both the neo-Fascist and leftist terrorists, one could do worse than to consider their groups as miniature versions of right and left-wing European political parties. The terrorist groups should be viewed as parties of the sort the French political scientist Maurice Duverger many years ago labeled devotee parties, parties of militants.

The revolutionary are also distinguishable from the neo-Fascist terrorists by virtue of their prior political involvements. To the extent the terrorists were reported to have had any previous political experiences these corresponded overwhelmingly to the ideological orientations of their respective terrorist groups. Revolutionary terrorists tended to come from the extra-parliamentary movements or the PCI, while many of the neo-Fascists were drawn from the MSI and its youth organizations. There were very few individuals who moved from Left to Right or Right to Left as they drifted into terrorist activities; there were fewer still who moved to the extremes after involvements in parties of the center. Thus, to the degree the terrorist population was composed of people with a record of prior political affiliation, the experiences they had as a consequence were ones that served to radicalize their political outlooks.

For the already mentioned 13 per cent of the terrorists who were related to one another, there are differences that also distinguish Left from Right. Not only was the frequency of the family tie more prevalent among the leftists, but the nature of the relationship was different. Where such a link was reported among the neo-Fascists, it was the sibling relationship that predominated, with brothers usually found among the members of these overwhelmingly male bands. For the revolutionary formations, the most common type of family tie was the marital one.

The picture that emerges from this analysis is one of segmentation. In general, the neo-Fascist and revolutionary terrorists came from different localities, although they converged in the big cities, were drawn largely from different social strata, and had prior political experience that divided them along left-right lines. And to the extent it could be measured, at least some of these violent individuals were attracted to their terrorist groups as the result of ties to members of their families with whom they shared common political orientations.

Early Versus Late Terrorists: The Contagion Spreads

The long duration of the recent terrorist experience in Italy permits us to address a particularly intriguing question: Are the individuals likely to become terrorists after the experience has persisted over a number of years the same kind as those attracted to the violent groups at its beginning? Or, are the founders and initiators of terrorism somehow different from those that followed them? Along with other forms of violent behavior, terrorism is often said to be contagious. But if this is so, does the contagion infect the same kinds of highly susceptible population groups over and over again, or does its persistence over time have the effect of expanding or spreading it to new and previously immune segments of the population?

At a minimum, latecomers to terrorist activities would be aware of the successes and failures of terrorist violence, as well as the personal fates of those who preceded them. They would be in a better position than the first generation to accurately judge the costs, risks and opportunities involved.

But does this awareness have any consequences so far as the particular kinds of people who get caught up in terrorism?

In the Italian case, the relevant year for making a distinction between newcomers and latecomers is 1977. As we have observed, by that year many of the first generation of revolutionary and neo-Fascist terrorists had been apprehended and brought to trial. Their organizations had been dissolved or severely crippled by the Italian authorities. Yet during 1977, the country witnessed the re-ignition of violence at a level that was not to subside until the early 1980s. A largely new generation of terrorist recruits and organizations left their mark. In what ways, if any, did the individuals identified as terrorists in 1977 and after differ from their predecessors?

Before proceeding to address this question, we should make clear that a generational replacement in the composition of the terrorist ranks indeed occurred. Some interpretations of the terrorist phenomenon emphasize not change but continuity. This view has it that 1968 and 1969 were the crucial years. Individuals attracted to terrorism over the next decade were formed politically by this period of mass student and worker protest. It was the formative political experience in their lives. For some, the impact of the "culture of 1968" was almost immediate; it resulted very rapidly in their decision to engage in terrorism. For others, the effect was delayed. After a long period in the extraparliamentary movements, they turned to violence in the aftermath of the 1976 parliamentary elections for reasons we have already discussed.

If the path to terrorism was begun by a single dramatic experience, we would expect that the ages of the terrorists at the time of their identification by the authorities would rise the more distant in time they were from the events of 1968–69.

In general, the evidence does not support this interpretation. As may be observed (see Table 5.3), of the 2,512 individuals in the terrorist population, 46 per cent were under the age of 16 in 1969. Eighteen per cent were less than 11 years old when the 'hot autumn' occurred. In other words, close to half the population of terrorists was too young to have taken a direct part in the turbulent events of 68–69. Even if we confine the analysis to the left-wing terrorists, the segment of the population really intended to be covered by the interpretation, the outcome is not altered. In fact, the left-wing terrorists were actually younger in 1969 than were the neo-Fascists. Of the 1,763 leftists in the population, 853 (or 64 per cent) were under 16 in 1969. Also, the terrorists arrested or identified in 1977 and after were significantly younger than those arrested or identified beforehand. These results offer persuasive evidence that a process of generational replacement or the diffusion of terrorism was underway.

The figures recorded in Table 5.4 reveal the differences between early and late adherents to terrorist groups. The principal understanding to be

TABLE 5.3
Age Distribution of Italian Terrorists in 1969

Age	Number of Terrorists	Per Cent
1 to 5	17	1
6 to 10	417	17
11 to 15	732	29
16 to 20	556	22
21 to 25	295	12
26 to 30	131	5
31 to 35	56	2
36 to 40	42	2
41 to 45	31	1
46 to 50	26	1
51 and above	219	9
Total	2512	100

derived from these data is that there occurred an expansion of terrorism to wider segments of Italian society as the episode progressed. Instead of a repetitive process with the new generation(s) of terrorists simply recapitulating the institutional affiliations and social backgrounds of the early ones, in general, the evidence suggests that terrorist groups were able to broaden and expand, not merely deepen their appeal, the longer the experience continued.

First, while the initial wave of terrorists was predominantly male, the later one included a substantial female presence. If we consider the terrorists' origins by looking at their places of birth, the second generation over-represents people who were born in smaller communities (under 100,000) as well as in Rome, the southern regions and outside the country. Geographically then, it appears as if the terrorists' roots spread from northern and central Italy to the South and out from the big cities to smaller communities the longer terrorism persisted. However, when we compare the two generations by their places of adult residence, rather than their birthplaces, some interesting changes emerge. Here the later generation appears somewhat less geographically dispersed than the first. The latecomers were more likely to have lived in the big cities of Turin, Milan, Genoa, Rome and Naples than their predecessors. This pattern suggests that the individuals drawn to terrorism later were far more mobile, taken as a group, than were members of the initial wave. Thus, whatever terrorist infection

TABLE 5.4
Differences Between Early (1970-1976) and Late (1977-1984) Italian
Terrorists

	Sex		
Group	Male	Female	Total
Early	449 (23.8)*	50 (11.2)	499
Late	1441 (76.2)	395 (88.8)	1836
Total	1890	445	2335

$\chi^2 = 32.86$ $p < .001$ $df = 1$ $\phi^2 = .12$

	Birthplace (Region)					
Group	North	Center	Rome	South	Foreign Born	Total
Early	156 (31.0)	50 (34.0)	37 (16.7)	58 (18.7)	5 (11.9)	306
Late	348 (69.0)	97 (66.0)	184 (83.3)	252 (81.3)	37 (88.1)	918
Total	504	147	221	310	42	1224

$\chi^2 = 34.31$ $p < .001$ $df = 4$ $\tau_b = .13$

	Birthplace (Size of Community)				
Group	Small Community	Medium City	Big City	Foreign Born	Total
Early	86 (19.5)	109 (28.2)	119 (24.0)	5 (11.9)	319
Late	354 (80.5)	227 (71.8)	377 (76.0)	37 (88.1)	1054
Total	440	386	496	42	1364

$\chi^2 = 11.88$ $p < .001$ $df = 3$ $\tau_b = -.02$

TABLE 5.4 (continued)
Differences Between Early (1970–1976) and Late (1977–1984) Italian
Terrorists

Place of residence (Region)

Group	North	Center	Rome	South	Foreign Born	Total
Early	273 (22.6)	60 (26.1	80 (14.0)	57 (22.5)	1 (33.3)	471
Late	935 (77.4)	170 (73.9)	492 (86.0)	196 (77.5)	2 (66.7)	1795
Total	1208	230	572	253	3	2266

$\chi^2 = 23.15$ $p < .001$ $df = 4$ $\tau_b = .047$

Place of residence (Size of Community)

Group	Small Community	Medium City	Big City	Foreign Born	Total
Early	52 (21.7)	136 (26.1)	285 (18.9)	1 (33.3)	474
Late	188 (78.3)	386 (73.9)	1226 (81.1)	2 (66.7)	1805
Total	240	522	1556	3	2276

$\chi^2 = 3.91$ $p < .04$ $df = 3$ $\phi^2 = .043$

Type of Family Relationship

Group	Marital	Sibling	Parental	Other	Total
Early	16 (11.8)	26 (18.7)	5 (41.7)	4 (22.2)	51
Late	120 (88.2)	113 (81.3)	7 (58.3)	14 (77.8)	254
Total	136	139	12	18	305

$\chi^2 = 8.54$ $p < .036$ $df = 3$ $\tau_b = .132$

TABLE 5.4 (continued)
Differences Between Early (1970-1976) and Late (1977-1984) Italian
Terrorists

Prior Political Party Affiliation

Group	Left	Center	Right	Total
Early	19 (30.2)	3 (75.0)	63 (73.3)	85
Late	44 (69.8)	1 (25.0)	23 (26.7)	68
Total	63	4	86	153

$\chi^2 = 27.98$ p < .001   df = 2 $\tau_b = -.41$

Extraparliamentary Movement Affiliation

Group	Left	Right	Total
Early	39 (11.4)	149 (85.6)	188
Late	302 (88.6)	25 (14.4)	327
Total	341	174	515

χ^2 270.43   p < .001   df = 1 $\phi^2 = .72$

Age At Time of Identification

Group	15-19	20-24	25-29	30-34	35-39	40-44	45-49	50+	Total
Early	27 (17.6)	150 (19.7)	117 (18.5)	62 (18.7)	31 (24.8)	24 (41.4)	22 (68.8)	34 (72.3)	467
Late	126 (82.4)	511 (80.3)	514 (81.5)	269 (81.3)	94 (75.2)	34 (58.6)	10 (31.3)	13 (27.7)	1671
Total	153	761	631	331	125	58	32	47	2138

$\chi^2 = 134.56$ p < .001   df = 7 $\tau_b = .102$

TABLE 5.4 (continued)
Differences Between Early (1970–1976) and Late (1977–1984) Italian
Terrorists

Occupation

Group	Criminal, Subprole-tarian	Student	Worker	Military Police	White Collar Impiegato	Small Business
Early	11 (17.5)	74 (21.1)	45 (12.7)	27 (52.9)	25 (11.5)	27 (46.6)
Late	52 (82.5)	277 (78.9)	310 (87.3)	24 (47.1)	193 (88.5)	31 (53.4)
Total	63	351	355	51	218	58

Group	Teacher	Free Professional	Industrialist/ Business Manager/ Aristocrat	Housewife	Total
Early	14 (11.3)	38 (39.6)	23 (65.7)	1 (9.1)	285
Late	110 (88.7)	58 (60.4)	12 (34.3)	10 (90.9)	1077
Total	124	96	35	11	1362

$\chi^2 = 151.97$ $p < .001$ $df = 9$ $\tau_b = -.085$

Role in Terrorist Group

Group	Supporter	Regular	Leader	Total
Early	22 (4.7)	379 (23.5)	94 (37.3)	495
Late	443 (95.3)	1235 (76.5)	158 (62.7)	1836
Total	465	1614	252	2331

$\chi^2 = 119.48$ $p < .001$ $df = 2$ $\tau_b = .218$

* Percentages in parenthesis are column percents.

Source: Slann, Martin, and Bernard Schechterman, Multidimensional Terrorism
(Boulder, CO: Lynne Reinner Publishers, 1987) 85–87. Used with permission.

was transmitted from one generation of terrorists to the next, it was one spread from individuals likely to have been born and reared in the major metropolitan areas to those who were comparative newcomers.

Change in the terrorists' occupational backgrounds is also consistent with the interpretation of the infection spreading to progressively wider segments of the population. The overall pattern was for terrorism to expand from the upper to the lower strata of Italian society. Though not without qualification, the data indicate that significantly higher proportions of the first than the second generation came from upper status backgrounds as business managers, industrialists and the free professions. The first terrorist generation was also composed disproportionately of individuals with lower middle class occupational experiences as shopkeepers, salesmen and artisans, as well as of people with police and professional military backgrounds.

Though persons from these backgrounds were not missing from the later recruits, the latter included a far higher representation of manual workers, white collar employees and, to a lesser extent, subproletarians, than the pre-1977 terrorist population. Students, from both universities and secondary schools, make a relatively constant and large contribution to the terrorists' ranks. Although the level of student involvement remains roughly the same in the two periods, the same cannot be said for their teachers. The representation of university instructors and school teachers increases substantially from 1977 forward.

If we treat these data somewhat differently and regard students, teachers, and free professionals as "intellectuals" (that is, people who spend a fair amount of their working lives dealing with abstract ideas), the consequence is that their contribution to terrorist activities appears both high and constant. What becomes variable between the two periods is the representation of individuals with backgrounds in business and labor. In the first period business is over-represented while in the second labor is.

For those terrorists who were related to one another, the incidence of family ties is more common among members of the second generation. This result is explicable almost exclusively by the more frequent presence of married couples to be found among the later adherents to terrorist groups. We cannot be certain, but this phenomenon may have been the result of husbands encouraging their wives to join, a particularly intimate form of terrorist contagion.

The two time-based segments of our population also appear to have had somewhat different kinds of pre-terrorist political experiences. Prior membership in a conventional political party was more common among early than late terrorists. On the other hand, the latter were more likely to have been members of the extraparliamentary movements. The biographical records are incomplete, but we may speculate, nonetheless, that terrorism spread from individuals who were more likely to have exposures to con-

TABLE 5.5
Distribution of Terrorists by Time Period and Orientation

	Early (1970–1976)	Late (1977–1984)	Total
Neo–Fascist	293	279	572
Left	206	1557	1763
	499	1836	2335

ventional political party life to those whose involvements were more likely confined to the violent supportive movements and to individuals with no reported pre-terrorist political experiences.

Finally, the early and late terrorists are distinguishable on the basis of the roles they played once inside the terrorist organizations. The prevalence of individuals identified as "supporters", those who furnished logistical and other forms of assistance, increased dramatically among the late adherents. This finding may be the result of the terrorist groups, after 1976, developing a more complex organizational structure, as well as an increase in their recruitment of and appeal to part-timers, persons holding regular jobs whose commitments to the terrorist enterprise were likely less intense than the people identified as "regulars" or "leaders" in the newspaper accounts and court records.

At this stage of the analysis, the evidence points to an understanding of Italian terrorism that emphasized its diffusion to progressively broader segments of the population. There appear to have been changes of various kinds in the geographic, institutional and social settings from which the terrorists emerged. But to what extent were these changes simply an artifact of the differential representation of leftist and neo-Fascist terrorists in the two periods with which we are concerned?

As may be seen by looking at Table 5.5, a majority of pre-1977 terrorists were neo-Fascists while the preponderance of the later ones were revolutionary leftists. It may very well be that the early/late distinctions were more a product of the different composition of the terrorist population during the two periods of terrorist activity.

In order to determine whether or not this is the case, we partitioned the terrorist population into the following four categories: early right, late right, early left and late left. The relevant questions then become: Were the early neo-Fascists different from the late ones? And, were there any ways in which the early leftists differed from their political successors?

TABLE 5.6
Differences between Early (1970–1976) and Late (1977–1984) Neo-Fascist
Terrorists

Characteristics	Early to Late Change
Sex	Late more female χ^2 = 9.82, 1 df, p <.002, phi = .138
Age	Late younger χ^2 = 91.92, 7 df, p < .001, τ_b = −.363
Place of Birth (Region)	Late more Rome, less North and Center χ^2 = 108.19, 4 df, p < .001, λ =.471
Place of Birth (Size of Community)	Late more big city χ^2 = 30.83, 3 df, p < .01, τ_b = .251
Place of Residence (Region)	Late more Rome, less North and Center χ^2 = 218.76, 4 df, p < .001, λ = .618
Place of Residence (Size of community)	Late more big city χ^2 = 81.53, 3 df, p < .001, λ =.344
Role in Organization	Late more supporters χ^2 = 132.20, 2 df, p < .001, τ_b =−.438

In seeking to answer the first question, let us begin with the negative findings. There was no significant difference among the neo-Fascists concerning their occupational backgrounds. In both periods, they tended to come from the same lower middle and upper middle sectors of Italian society. In addition, they tended to be drawn from the same MSI based, right-wing political milieu. On the other hand, there were proportionately fewer late neo-Fascists who were reported to have had any previous political experiences before developing links with the terrorist groups. Last, the late neo-Fascists were no more or less likely to have been related to one another than the first collection.

If we focus on those variables (see Table 5.6) which do evoke meaningful differences, the case for terrorism spreading to wider segments of the population becomes far more ambiguous than it is when the entire terrorist population is considered. It is true that the later neo-Fascists were substantially younger than members of the earlier group. The representation of women becomes higher, although it is never very high among the neo-Fascists. Also, the proportion of "supporters" relative to "regulars" and "leaders" grows in the second wave. Yet when we look at their places of birth and adult residence, the case for an expansion of neo-Fascist terrorism to broader segments of society weakens. Measured in terms of both where they were born and where they resided, the early neo-Fascists were a more geographically diverse group than the later ones.

Despite the fact they were able to reorganize and recruit a largely new generation of adherents, it is clear that after the mid-1970s, the neo-Fascists were a waning force. Their leaders' plans to provoke a coup d'état had been uncovered, publicized and defeated. The number of violent events for which they were responsible declined. In part, our findings reflect this decline. From a geographic perspective, we witness a concentration rather than an expansion of neo-Fascist terrorism between the two periods. As a group, the late neo-Fascists were more urbanized and Rome-centered than the early ones. However, when we consider the matter from a social or inter-personal perspective, there is some evidence of expansion as suggested by their age distribution, gender and level of presumed involvement in their respective organizations.

While neo-Fascist terrorism was waning in the second period, revolutionary terrorism was expanding. As measured by the number of violent attacks and in the number of adherents included in our population, terrorism from the left experienced dramatic growth. Logically then, we might expect this growth to be reflected in a wider diffusion of the infection than was true for the neo-Fascists.

Yet in some respects (see Table 5.7), the ways in which the growth of left-wing terrorism manifested itself in the the changing characteristics of the terrorists' backgrounds were not very different than the early to late changes in the makeup of the neo-Fascist formations. As with the latter, the second generation of leftists was younger than the first. It was also more heavily composed of "supporters". And a smaller proportion of the late than the early leftists were reported to have had prior memberships in conventional political parties.

There were some ways, however, in which the differences among leftists were unlike those exhibited by the neo-Fascists. The occupational back-grounds of the two leftist generations were meaningfully different. There are noticeable declines in the proportion of terrorists identified as free professionals and subproletarians, as well as a more modest decline in student representation. The proportions of manual workers, white collar clerks and teachers increases in the second generation. The effect of these changes, though, is hardly like that of the overall change in the terrorist population discussed earlier. While it is true that the second period leftist organizations were more successful in recruiting workers than the first, the clear pattern of terrorism spreading from high to low status in the Italian occupational structure now becomes unclear. This overall trend seems to have been more a product of the different mixes of neo-Fascists and revolutionaries

TABLE 5.7
Differences Between Early (1970-1976) and Late (1977-1984) Left-Wing
Terrorists

Characteristic	Early to Late Change
Age	Late younger $\chi^2 = 218.15$, 10 df, p < .001, $\tau_b = -.218$
Place of Residence (Region)	Late more Center and Rome, less South $\chi^2 = 15.16$, 4 df, p < .004, $\lambda = 0.0$
Occupation	Late more workers, clerks, teachers; less students, free professionals and subproletarians $\chi^2 = 25.04$, 8 df, p < .003, $\tau_b = -.251$
Previous Political Experience	Late more extraparliamentary movement; less political party membership $\chi^2 = 14.23$, 1 df, p < .001, $\tau_b = -.251$
Role in Organization	Late more supporters $\chi^2 = 30.57$, 2 df, p < .001, $\tau_b = -.127$

found in the two periods. The neo-Fascists, early and late, tended to come from higher status backgrounds than the leftists taken as a whole.

When we consider the issue from a geographic perspective, we are unable to discern any significant generational changes in the leftists' places of birth. Late leftists were no more or less likely to have been born in the South or outside the big cities, for example, than the early ones. However, there is a discernible early to late shift in the revolutionaries' places of residence, with the second generation more likely to be found in the central regions and Rome. But the representation of terrorists from the heavily industrialized North remained high over both periods. The case for an expansion of terrorism to new and different segments of society is also attenuated by the facts that there are proportionately fewer residents of the southern regions among the late leftists and that there were no meaningful early/late differences related to the size of the communities in which they were born.

So far as the left-wing terrorists' gender is concerned, rather surprisingly the late leftists did not show a significant increase in women members as against the early groups. There was a change in the kinds of women who appear in the second period. The data indicate an increase in the proportion of married women. Furthermore, second generation women were more likely to have played leadership roles in the terrorist groups than were females belonging to the first generation.

Summary

As is evident by now, the revolutionary leftists and the neo-Fascists were, in several ways, different kinds of people. And it was the differential contribution of the two groups to the terrorist population in the pre- and post-1977 periods that made for the clear pattern of Italian terrorism's expansion to new and wider segments of the society.

Yet despite the impact of the differential mix of neo-Fascists and leftists in the two periods, there were still several ways in which the terrorist infection spread. Irrespective of political orientation, the late terrorists were younger, had less conventional political experience and appeared in the aggregate less thoroughly involved in the organizations than their predecessors.

The spread of terrorism to these new elements may have been caused by the new crisis Italy went through in 1977—a crisis, as we described it, set-off by a combination of galloping inflation and rising unemployment. The effect of the crisis likely made large numbers of previously apolitical young people susceptible to the terrorist infection. The susceptibility was likely heightened by their awareness of the widely publicized exploits of the earlier terrorists, as well as personal interaction with those still active remnants from the earlier contingent that had evaded detection by the authorities.

Terrorist organizations may recruit new members not only by widening their appeal to previously unengaged segments of the population, but also by drawing on the same social bases from which the original adherents emerged. This form of contagion was also at work in Italy. In general, people tend to talk politics, even violent politics, with those with whom they agree. In the Italian case we have found instances where the terrorist infection was transmitted among members of the same primary group: families of leftist and neo-Fascist persuasion. In other cases, the late recruits came from the same or similar social and political backgrounds as the early ones. Students were heavily represented among both early and late revolutionary terrorists. Similarly, the two generations of neo-Fascists surfaced from the same occupational contexts and right-wing political milieu.

The recruitment of terrorists in Italy occurred as the result of both a spread or expansion to different sectors of society and as a contagion to individuals from highly susceptible circumstances. But in both cases, we cannot help but be impressed by the large number of people with no deeply held ethnic, religious or racial differences who were willing to take up arms against their own democratic political order.

Notes

1. See for example, Colin Smith, *Carlos: Portrait of a Terrorist* (New York: Holt, Rinehart and Winston, 1976); Jillian Becker, *Hitler's Children* (New York: J.B. Lippincott, 1977).

2. See for example, Alessandro Silj, *Never Again Without a Rifle* (New York: Harz Publishers, 1979); Giordano Bruno Guerri, *Patrizio Peci: io l'infame* (Milan: Mondadori, 1983).

3. Walter Laquer, *Terrorism* (Boston: Little, Brown, 1977) pp. 133–148.

4. Charles Russell and Bowman Miller, "Profile of a Terrorist," in Lawrence Freedman and Yonah Alexander (eds.), *Perspectives on Terrorism* (Wilmington, Del.: Scholarly Resources, 1983) pp. 45–60.

5. In addition to *La Stampa* and *La Repubblica* the following court record were examined: for the neo-Fascist New Order, National Vanguard and National Revolutionary Front and Third Position; Luigi Gennaro, Giudice Istruttore, *Ordinanza/ Sentenza* N 2736/80A (Tribunale di Roma); Corte D'Assise d'appello di Firenze, *Sentenza* (December 12, 1978), *Sentenza* (April 9, 1976) and *Sentenza* (November 11, 1977). For the revolutionary groups—Partisan Action Groups, Armed Proletarian Nuclei, Red Brigades, Front Line, Worker Autonomy and related bands—the records were: Francesco Amato, Giudice Istruttore, *Ordinanza/Sentenza* 231/83 (Tribunale civile e penale di Milano); Giudice Istruttore, *Ordinanza* N 228/81 (Tribunale civile e penale di Milano); Publicco Ministero, *Requisitoria* N 921/80F (Procura della Repubblica in Milano); Ferdinando Imposimato, Giudice Istruttore, *Ordinanza/ Sentenza* N 54/80A (Tribunale di Roma); Giudice Istruttore, *Ordinanze/Sentenza* 490/81F (Tribunale civile e penale di Milano) 1; Corte D'Assise di Torino, *Sentenza* N 17/81 (July 28, 1981); Corte D'Assise D'Appello di Torino, *Sentenza* N 2/83; and Corte D'Assise di Firenze, (April 24, 1983).

6. Fabio Mussi, *Zangheri: Bologna '77* (Rome: Riuniti, 1978) pp. 17–26; Ezio Mauro, *Novelli: vivere a Torino* (Rome: Riuniti, 1980) pp. 15–17.

7. Bruce Hoffman, *Right-Wing Terrorism in Europe* (Santa Monica, CA.: Rand Corporation, 1982) p. 15.

— lack of direction & goals. — *your 2 students*

6
TERRORIST ATTACKS

Now that we have some understanding of who the terrorists were, it is appropriate to analyze what they did. The focus of this chapter is on terrorist events. In the preceding chapter, we maintained that a review of the biographies of terrorist celebrities, terrorist leaders who attracted great doses of personal publicity, did not provide an adequate basis for understanding the sociology of terrorists. In the same sense, a focus on a few spectacular acts of violence, a massacre or the assassination of a former prime minister, does not provide us with a clear picture of terrorist activity in general. Accordingly, our attention will be on the overall pattern of terrorist attacks committed from 1969 through 1982.

The discussion will be divided in two parts. First, we will describe the general characteristics of these violent events: when and where they occurred, which groups committed them and who the victims were. The second section will seek to explain the causes of the events. In particular, we will explore the extent to which the incidence of terrorist violence was related to various social, economic and political changes Italy was experiencing as the events unfolded.

When, Where and Who

The figures in Table 6.1 record the incidence of terrorist attacks in Italy by year from 1969 through 1982. The table reports three types of events. Acts of political violence—fights, beatings, assaults and other forms of open political clashes or street corner violence committed by terrorist groups—constitute the first type. In this instance, it is not the nature of the act itself, but the nature of the group engaged in it that provides the basis of the classification. The second and third types of events are terrorist attacks, planned acts of violence against people or property committed by terrorist groups. The distinction between the second and third indicators is based

TABLE 6.1
Political Terrorism in Italy, 1969-1982

	A Acts of Political Violence				B Terrorist Attacks (Responsibility Not Claimed)				C Terrorist Attacks (Responsibility Claimed)		
	Left	Neo-Fascist	Other	Sum	Left	Neo-Fascist	Unknown	Sum	Left	Neo-Fascist	Sum
1969	10	148	52	210	1	148	63	214	1	16	17
1970	1	286	31	318	8	202	20	230	4	2	6
1971	17	460	38	515	3	258	34	295	6	16	22
1972	39	402	32	473	18	211	28	257	31	15	46
1973	20	345	18	383	20	192	15	227	11	27	38
1974	65	363	2	430	49	211	21	281	32	43	75
1975	44	154	1	199	76	117	13	206	48	14	62
1976	63	110	3	176	157	149	87	393	106	10	116
1977	216	168	23	407	533	218	360	1111	244	43	287
1978	472	279	30	781	480	367	381	1228	638	78	716
1979	143	138	8	289	380	269	396	1045	659	146	805
1980	46	45	18	109	41	161	228	430	222	72	294
1981	26	23	8	57	23	33	116	172	115	21	136
1982	11	4	0	15	3	9	54	66	71	21	92
Total	1173	2925	264	4362	1972	2545	1816	6153	2188	524	2712

Source: Donatella della Porta and Maurizio Rossi, Cifre crudelli: bilancio del terrorismi italiani (Bologna: Instituo Cattaneo, 1983) pp. 18-19. Reprinted by permission.

on whether or not the group committing the attack publicly claimed responsibility for it. If no such claim was made, it was the authorities that assigned the blame. Last, the table records the events under each indicator based on the political orientation of the groups responsible for their commission.

The first observation we may derive from the table is one we have mentioned before. Terrorist activity in Italy did not follow a linear path of development. Instead, we find relatively distinct periods. The frequency of terrorist events is relatively moderate between 1969 and 1976 and then escalates dramatically in 1977 only to decline equally dramatically in 1980 and after as the impact of government measures to repress the terrorist organizations is felt.

The data also indicate that after 1976 there was a greater willingness on the part of the relevant groups to claim responsibility for their deeds. As may be seen, this trend applies to both the revolutionary and neo-Fascist organizations, although, in general, the former were consistently more willing to reveal their identities than the latter. Thus, after 1976, the terrorist groups displayed a greater boldness, both in terms of the frequency of their attacks and in their willingness to claim responsibility for them.

There was also a meaningful change in the political coloration of the groups committing the violence. As discussed earlier, the initial period of terrorist activity was dominated by the neo-Fascists, while after 1976 it was largely the product of the leftist organizations.

But in neither period were the attacks distributed uniformly throughout Italy. Geographically, some areas were the sites of a high level of terrorist violence while a few remained largely immune to the phenomenon.

The information recorded in the first two columns of Table 6.2 concerns attacks, responsibility for which was claimed by either neo-Fascist or leftist groups. Accordingly, these data may be biased towards attacks that took place after 1976. The data reported in the third column labeled "total political attacks" are a composite of attacks on people or property, as well as attacks resulting in death or injury, irrespective of whether responsibility for their commission was claimed, or assigned by the authorities or whether their perpetrators remained unknown.

On the basis of all three measures, Lazio, the region in which Rome is located, stands out as the most frequent site of terrorist violence. After Lazio, it is the North in general and those regions, Lombardy (Milan) and Piedmont (Turin), in which there are major cities that suffered the most. In fact, there is a positive, though imperfect, relationship between the presence of a large city in a region and the level of its susceptibility to political violence. On the other side of the ledger, those regions—the Aosta Valley in the North and Molise and Basilcata in the South—with high rural populations experienced low levels of violence.

TABLE 6.2
The Regional Distribution of Terrorist Attacks, 1969-1982

Region	Neo-Fascist	Leftist	Total Political Attacks
Piedmont	16	341	1193
Aosta Valley	0	2	3
Lombardy	108	317	2392
Trentino-Alto Adige	33	20	154
Venento	18	247	654
Friuli-Venezio Giulia	6	17	157
Liguria	13	95	269
North	194 (37.5%)	1041 (49.2%)	4822 (36.5%)
Emilia Romagna	16	114	713
Tuscany	11	119	428
Umbria	3	15	73
Marches	4	19	69
Center	34 (6.5%)	267 (12.6%)	1283 (9.7%)
Lazio	2 (49.9%)	607 (28.7%)	4737 (35.9%)
Abruzzi	4	6	75
Molise	0	0	8
Campania	25	91	743
Puglia	2	23	329
Basilcata	1	2	21
Calabria	2	16	479
Sicily	28	18	419
Sardinia	5	47	267
South	67 (12.9%)	203 (9.6%)	2341 (17.8%)
Totals	517 (100.0%)	2113 (100.0%)	13183 (100.0%)

Sources: Mauro Galleni (ed.), Rapporto Sul Terrorismo (Milan: Rizzoli, 1981) pp. 119-124, 247-288; Attentati E Violenze in Italia Nel 1981 (Rome: Direzione PCI, 1982); Attentati E Violenze in Italia Nel 1982 (Rome: Direzione PCI, 1982).

There are also meaningful variations between the regions in the types of terrorist activity they exhibited. The southern ones, with the exception of Campania (Naples) did not experience many events where responsibility was claimed by a particular terrorist group. Yet, if we consider the total volume of attacks, the *Mezzogiorno* appears to have been a far from tranquil locale. Similarly, Piedmont (Turin) and the Veneto were hard hit by attacks claimed by the revolutionary groups but were only infrequently the sites for violence claimed by the neo-Fascist ones.

The fact that those regions containing major metropolitan areas were the sites of much violence does not mean that terrorism was not widely dispersed throughout Italy. As the data make clear, most regions experienced at least a moderate level of violent events. The matter of the relationship between the regions' differential susceptibility to terrorist attack and their social, economic and political characteristics is one we intend to address shortly.

To this point, our concern has been with when and where the violent events occurred. However, any analysis of these events would be lacking if it did not consider their victims.

In the period 1969–1982 a total of 1,119 people were either injured or killed (351) as the result of terrorist violence.[1] This number does not include members of terrorist groups who were killed or injured in the course of their operations. If we consider the question chronologically, the worst years were clearly 1969, 1974 and 1980. This is true because of the heavy toll taken by the *stragi* or massacres which occurred during these years. If we exclude these events, terrorism only becomes a significant source of death and injury in 1977 and after.

From the victims' point of view, it would not seem to matter much whether one is murdered or maimed by leftist or neo-Fascist terrorists. Nevertheless, for observers seeking to assess the relative impact of revolutionary and right-wing terrorism, the matter is of some importance. According to figures compiled by della Porta and Rossi and reported in Table 6.3, the neo-Fascist groups caused a majority of both deaths and injuries over the course of Italy's terrorist experience. This finding furnishes additional evidence that, as compared to other western democracies with terrorist experiences of their own, Italy stands out by virtue of the virulence of its rightist violence.

In understanding political terrorism in Italy, it is of some importance to determine not only the terrorists' backgrounds but also those of their principal victims. What sorts of people were killed as the result of terrorist operations?

As the data displayed in Table 6.4 disclose, by far the most frequent fatal victims of terrorist attacks were members of Italy's various police agencies (102). If we add to this number the judges and magistrates who

TABLE 6.3
Victims of Terrorist Violence by Groups Responsible

	Deaths and Injuries	Deaths*
Neo-Fascist	758 (68%)	186 (53%)
Leftist	360 (32%)	164 (47%)
	1118 (100%)	350 (100%)

*One murder remains unresolved and the figures do not
include deaths or injuries suffered by the terrorists
themselves.

TABLE 6.4
Occupations of Persons Killed as the Result of Terrorist Violence 1969-1982

Occupation	Number Killed	Per Cent
Terrorists	51	12.7
Police Officers and Bodyguards	102	25.0
Magistrates	11	3.0
Journalists	1	0.2
Government and Political Party Officials	6	1.0
Business Managers and Owners	13	3.0
Manual Workers and Clerks	48	12.0
Students	47	12.0
University Instructors	9	2.0
Physicians	9	2.0
Housewives and Domestics	25	6.0
Salesmen and Artisans	22	5.0
Farmers and Peasants	8	2.0
Pensioners	15	4.0
Others	42	10.0
Total	409	100.0

Sources: Mauro Galleni (ed.), Rapporto Sul Terrorismo (Milan: Rizzoli, 1981)
p. 50; Attentati E Violenze in Italia Nel 1981 (Rome: Direzione PCI, 1982);
Attentatati E Violenze in Italia Nel 1982 (Rome: Direzione PCI, 1982).

were also murdered and consider that 51 terrorists were killed during the
experience, we have explained more than 38 per cent of the deaths involved.
Thus, if we measure the severity of the experience simply in terms of the
number of deaths involved, Italian terrorism appears as a lethal conflict
between the terrorists and those legally charged to repress their activities.

Furthermore, the proportion of police and terrorist deaths relative to other terrorism caused deaths increased substantially in 1981–82, as the authorities were successful in destroying the terrorist organizations.

If we consider the fact that 123 people died as a result of the neo-Fascist massacres, events where the victims were random bystanders rather than individuals deliberately targeted for assassination, another conclusion can be reached. The leftist revolutionary groups initially sought to carry out "exemplary" actions directed against executives employed by Fiat, Sit-Siemens and other large scale business firms. The intent was to inspire the working class, to raise it to revolutionary consciousness. The terrorists then changed tactics and swore to attack the "heart of the state" by waging campaigns of violence against prominent political figures. Likewise, spokesmen for the second generation of neo-Fascist groups committed themselves to attacking the state apparatus. With these thoughts in mind, a striking feature of the figures reported in Table 6.4 is the small number of individuals who, by the most liberal standards, might be considered, in some sense, part of the establishment and who fell victim to the terrorists. The total number of government and party political officials, business managers, journalists, university professors, and physicians who they murdered comes to 38. This figure is a reflection of the failure of the terrorists to make good their threats and achieve their objectives. Most of those killed as a result of terrorist activities were not members of an Italian establishment, nor did they represent the "heart of the state". Instead, most victims came from quite ordinary backgrounds.

Explaining the Sources of Terrorist Violence

In the introductory chapter, we discussed various interpretations of the terrorist experience proposed by Italian social scientists. As against accounts that viewed the experience as the product of international conspiracies or Italy's own political history, these putative explanations emphasize relatively recent changes in the country's social, economic and political characteristics. Is it possible to determine which, if any, of these interpretations fits the available evidence?

For several decades now, social scientists have sought to explain the incidence of political violence within nations by measuring the extent to which just such sorts of changes precede or coincide with their manifestations.[2] For the most part, however, these studies have sought to explain, not terrorism, but large-scale forms of domestic political violence: revolutions, civil wars, guerrilla insurgencies and the like. It is not clear if these statistically based explanatory strategies are applicable to terrorist experiences. One observer has asked whether it is possible to explain the activities of the Symbionese Liberation Army in the United States through an analysis of the demographic characteristics of the state of California? That is, in the case of terrorism, where both the number of terrorists and the number of violent acts for which they are responsible are usually quite small, it is useless to rely on broad measures of the economic or social attributes of the populations residing in the areas where terrorist attacks occur as means of explaining them.[3]

This logic may apply to cases where the number of terrorist events is small, the kidnapping of a newspaper heiress and the assassination of a school administrator, but is it equally true in the Italian case? Here we are not dealing with a handful of violent acts, but with more than 13,000 that occurred over a 15 year period and were distributed over an entire country. Potentially at least, it would seem that Italian terrorism lends itself to this form of analysis.

In order to determine if it does, and if the interpretations proposed but not tested by Italian social scientists can account for the incidence of terrorist violence, we conducted a series of multiple regression analyses on the data available to us. First, we treated the three regional distributions of terrorist events shown in Table 6.2 as dependent variables. We then sought to explain the regional variations in the frequency of these events by measuring the extent to which the level of, or changes in, different social, cultural, economic and political characteristics within the regions varied with the volume of their incidence of terrorist violence. The characteristics of the regions we measured and treated as independent variables were as follows: 1) the contemporary population characteristics including their overall size, degree of urbanization, rates of increase (or decrease) and the distribution of their labor forces by employment sector (including unemployment rates); 2) the degree of social and cultural change they experienced as reflected by voting returns for the 1974 and 1981 referendums on divorce and abortion law challenges; 3) indicators of social and economic problems as reflected by regional crime rates and hours of work lost as the result of labor conflicts; and 4) the level of support enjoyed by the Communist Party (PCI), various parties of the extreme left and the Italian Social Movement (MSI) at all parliamentary elections between 1968 and 1983. In addition, membership figures for the PCI, its Youth Federation (FGCI) and the major trade union federation, the General Confederation of Italian Workers (CGIL), were recorded for each region at different time intervals from 1970 through 1980.[4] In evaluating their impacts on the frequency of terrorist events, these variables were measured both by the degree of change they displayed over the duration of the terrorist experience and by their average magnitude or size during this period. Finally, we also sought to determine the extent to which the number of attacks carried out by the leftist revolutionary and neo-Fascist groups in the regions during the same period (1969–1982) were reciprocal or were independent of one another.

With one exception, our initial efforts to predict the levels of terrorist events in the regions, using all three measures of them, were unsuccessful. None of the independent variables hypothesized by Italian social scientists and operationalized for this analysis succeeded in explaining a significant proportion of the violence, leftist, neo-Fascist or total. The one exception to these negative findings was the relationship between the leftist and neo-Fascist attacks themselves. Here we discovered a strong and positive link ($R^2 = .725$) between these two measures of terrorist violence. Regions which experienced a high number of leftist attacks tended to be those where there had occurred a high incidence of attacks claimed by the neo-Fascist groups. In other words, leftist and rightist violent acts seem to have provoked each other.

In observing the results of this initial series of step-wise multiple regression analyses, we noticed a geographically distinct pattern to the standardized residuals resulting from the calculations. The residuals for the northern regions of Piedmont, the Aosta Valley, Lombardy and Trentino-Alto Adige were more widely dispersed than those of all the other regions north of Rome (Lazio). The pattern for southern Italy, including Sicily and Sardinia, also appeared distinct. Furthermore, the residuals for Rome (Lazio) were unlike those for the rest of the country. These results suggested that regional differences were at work in accounting for the different frequencies of our three measures of terrorist violence. In other words, independent variables had different consequences in different sections of the country.

We are hardly the first observers to have noticed the importance of regionalism as an independent force in understanding Italian political life. The literature abounds with references to the historical role regionalism has played in affecting different forms of Italian political behavior. At any rate, because of the regional pattern we discovered, we constructed dummy variables by dividing Italy into the following regions: North (Piedmont, Aosta Valley, Lombardy and Trentino-Alto Adige), Center (all the other regions north of Lazio), South and Lazio (Rome). Given this procedure, we were able to assess the influence of regionalism and the other independent variables on the frequency of terrorist events while also controlling for the aberrant characteristics of Lazio.

When Lazio is controlled and the other regions entered as dummies into the regression equations, some interesting findings emerge. There are positive and statistically meaningful relationships between the frequency of total political violence in the regions and their average unemployment rates; the hours of work lost as the result of strikes; the average vote received by parties of the extreme left and those to the left of the PCI; and average membership in the PCI's Youth Federation, the FGCI. Thus, in addition to the independent influence of the regions, those areas of Italy where there was high unemployment and labor conflict, as well as sections of the country where the radical left did well at the polls and where the Young Communists were strong, exhibited substantially higher levels of total political violence than other parts of Italy.

Intuitively, these findings make considerable sense, particularly if we regard the unemployment rate as affecting young people disproportionately—that segment of the population from which the terrorist organizations were able to recruit so many of their members. We might conceive of voting for the radical left parties, joining the Young Communist Federation and committing acts of political terrorism as a repetoire of political responses to an economic environment of high unemployment and labor unrest. Our analysis then provides some support for those interpretations of Italian terrorism which emphasize the role of "social marginalization" or economically-based discontent as a causal factor.[5]

However, the same variables are not equally successful in predicting the frequency of attacks claimed by leftist and neo-Fascist groups. So far as the former are concerned, the percentage of the work force in search of jobs makes a marginal contribution to understanding the frequency of attacks. But it is the overtly political variables that exhibit the strongest capacity. There are, in other words, strong relationships between the incidence of leftist violence and the level of electoral support received by the parties of the extreme left and the average size of the FGCI's membership within the regions. Terrorist attacks claimed by neo-Fascist groups are predicted only by the magnitude of the radical left vote. The latter then is the only variable that bears a substantive link to all three measures of political terrorism. Again, the reasons for the consistent contribution of this variable are not hard to adduce.

During most of the period with which we have been concerned, the parties of the extreme left (e.g., the Democratic Proletarians) represented the electoral manifestations of the revolutionary political movements— Manifesto, Potere Operaio, Lotta Continua—that emerged from the struggles of 1968-69. And it was from these movements that the revolutionary terrorist organizations drew many of their members, particularly after 1976. Thus, those areas in which the radical left parties did well at the polls were also ones that likely contained a large number of the movements' supporters and hence individuals susceptible to the appeals of terrorist violence.

But why the linkage between the radical left vote and the frequency of neo-Fascist attacks? The answer may be that neo-Fascist violence both was provoked by the presence of the extreme left in large numbers and itself acted as provocation for leftist violence in a cycle of mutually reinforcing extremism. It should be recalled that the only variable that bore a significant relationship to the incidence of neo-Fascist attacks before we introduced

TABLE 6.5
Accounting for the Frequency of Terrorist Violence in the Italian Regions

Total Political Attacks			
Constant	4209.50	Constant	2727.82
North	-4043.73	North	-3301.83
Center	-4347.56	Center	-3969.44
South	-4242.60	South	-4041.69
Total Crime	0.002*	Mean Radical Left Vote	980.58
Hours Lost Labor Conflict	0.067	Mean MSI Vote	45.72*
Per Cent Unemployed	2.19	Mean Young Communist Membership	0.058
R^2	.98	R^2	.95

Total Neo-Fascist Attacks		Leftist Attacks	
Constant	160.95	Constant	341.91
North	-169.45	North	-425.91
Center	-193.71	Center	-495.19
South	-200.46	South	-532.52
Mean MSI Vote	3.05*	Mean MSI Vote	-1.54*
Mean Radical Left Vote	35.04	Mean Radiacal Left Vote	194.56
Mean PCI Vote	-0.669*	Mean FGCI Membership	.0075
Mean PCI Membership	0.0002*		
Mean FGCI Membership	.002*		
R^2	.94	R^2	.85

*Not Significant

the regional dummies was the incidence of attacks carried out by the revolutionary groups.

In view of the explanations for terrorism hypothesized by various Italian social scientists, it is worthwhile mentioning what our analysis does not confirm. First, to the extent we were able to measure it, cultural change in Italian life was not associated with the incidence of terrorist act. Changes in the level of support for or opposition to civil divorce and abortion at the 1974 and 1981 national referendums were not linked to our three measures of terrorist violence. If vote returns on these occasions reflect attitudes towards the secularization of society, the influence of the Church and the role of the family, they do not explain terrorism.

Related to an interpretation which emphasizes the cultural secularization of Italian society are those interpretations which associate terrorism with the country's urbanization and correlative changes in the composition of its labor force. Religious to secular, rural to urban, agricultural to industrial followed by a growth in the service sector are all changes conventionally placed under the broader category of modernization. But our analysis does not support a view that identifies terrorism as an outgrowth of strains produced by the modernization of Italian society. Neither population growth (or decline) nor shifts in employment patterns in the regions between 1970 and 1980 censuses directly predict levels of political violence.

Another putative explanation for Italy's terrorist experience ascribes it to the "blocked" character of the country's political system, notably the dominant role played in it by the Christian Democratic party. Widespread frustration with the party's hold on power, it has been maintained, served to promote the violence as other avenues for political change appeared to be blocked. Such motivation was clearly relevant for the leftist and neo-Fascist terrorist organizations. Certainly they wanted to expel the Christian Democrats from power. And, as we have seen, the radical left's electoral support did predict the incidence of political violence.

Yet other indicators we used to measure the degree of popular dissatisfaction with the "blocked" political system were not successful in explaining the frequency of terrorist events. One reflection of dissatisfaction with Christian Democratic rule is support for the Communist party, the DC's principal antagonist. During the 1970s, particularly in the regional council elections of 1974 and the national balloting of 1976, the Communists enjoyed a dramatic increase in voter support. However, we found that the PCI's electoral strength was not related to the frequency of terrorist events. Neither the average level of voter support for the party at national elections between 1968 and 1983, nor changes in the level of its support during this period helped predict the frequency of violence in the regions.

Still another potential reflection of popular frustration with the "blocked" political system is a measure we have labeled 'electoral volatility.' Until the 1970s, the Italian electorate enjoyed the reputation of being among the most stable in the western democracies. The election-to-election gains and losses experienced by most political parties in the system were meager when compared to their counterparts elsewhere. The terrorist era coincided with a decline in this pattern of stability, a result perhaps of a process of generational change in the composition of the Italian electorate. As older age cohorts died and were replaced by younger postwar generations of voters, habitual levels of support for the different parties began to shift.

Our measure of 'electoral volatility' was based on the percentage of gains and losses experienced by the neo-Fascist Italian Social Movement, the Communists and the radical left parties at the parliamentary elections of 1968, 1972, 1976, 1979 and 1983. Since it reflects change at the right and left extremes of the party system and among parties that did not participate in coalition governments with the Christian Democrats, 'electoral volatility' should be particularly sensitive to opposition to the blocked status quo. Yet in spite of this logic, regions with high levels of 'electoral volatility' were not significantly more likely to have experienced a greater number of terrorist events than those displaying less volatility. If terrorism was caused by a reaction against the blockage in the political system, it is not reflected by these findings.

* * *

In sum, when we take regional differences into consideration and when Lazio (Rome) is controlled, the only structural factors that predict the incidence of political violence are economic ones. High rates of unemployment and manifestations of labor conflict were linked to the overall measure of political violence, with the former also related to the level of leftist attacks. It should be born in mind, however, that the various measures of social and cultural change we employed coincided with, rather than preceded, the terrorist events. It is possible, of course, that had we been able to measure these developments before the outbreak of terrorism, the results might have been different.

What our data do suggest is an explanation for the incidence of terrorism which stresses the distinctive features of the regions themselves and calls attention to the presence of large numbers of voters of the extreme left as indispensable ingredients. But in a sense, in reporting the tie between large numbers of radical left voters and frequent terrorist events, we may be looking at two side of the same coin.

Notes

1. Donatella della Porta and Maurizio Rossi, *Cifre crudelli: bilancio dei terrorismi italiana* (Bologna: Cattaneo, 1984) pp. 60–65.

2. See for example, Ted Gurr, *Why Men Rebel* (Princeton, N.J.: Princeton University Press, 1970).

3. Walter Laqueur, *Terrorism* (Boston: Little, Brown, 1977) pp. 142–143.

4. Data on population characteristics, employment and crime rates were taken from the *Annuario Statistico Italiano* 1975 and 1983 editions (Rome: Istituto Centrale di Statistica); regional figures on the number of hours lost as a result of labor

conflicts in 1974 were from, *Annuario di Statistiche Provinciali*, vol. 12 (Rome: Istituto Centrale di Statistica); PCI and FGCI membership data were taken from *Almanacco PCI '76* (Rome: PCI, 1976), Celso Ghini, *Il terremoto del 15 Giugno* (Milan: Feltrinelli, 1976) and *Partito Comunista Italiano 1981* (Rome: PCI, 1981); figures on CGIL membership in 1968 and 1974 were found in Aldo Amoretti, "Risultati e problemi del tesseramento e del finanziamento del sindicato," *Rassegna Sindicale Quaderni* 12:50 (1974) pp. 55–57. Regional voting returns were computed from data published in *La Stampa* and Howard Penniman (ed.), *Italy at The Polls: The Parliamentary Elections of 1976* (Washington, D.C.: American Enterprise Institute, 1977), and *Italy At The Polls: 1979* (Washington, D.C.: American Enterprise Institute, 1981). Results of the divorce and abortion referendums of 1974 and 1981 were taken from *La Stampa.*

5. Gianfranco Pasquino and Donatella della Porta, "Interpretations of Italian Left-Wing Terrorism," in Peter Merkl (ed.), *Political Violence and Terror* (Berkeley: University of California Press, 1986) pp. 169–188.

7

THE RESPONSE OF
THE STATE TO THE
TERRORIST THREAT

The democratic order in Italy has been preserved and domestic terrorism defeated, or at least reduced to marginal significance. Italy though, is not unique in having overcome a substantial terrorist threat. Turkey, Argentina and Uruguay, among others, were able to accomplish this task. But the price these countries paid to do it was a high one. It involved the abandonment of their democratic systems in favor of military rule and the suppression of constitutional guarantees of personal liberty. The Italian state was able to stop the terrorists without resorting to the authoritarian measures employed in these nations.

Given the interest of governments in various parts of the world in finding ways to overcome their own terrorist threats, the Italian success is of considerable relevance. There is a certain amount of irony in thinking the Italian government's performance might be worth emulating elsewhere. In the postwar era the Italian state has not enjoyed a high reputation for effectiveness, even among its own citizens. Indeed, many of the terrorists believed their objectives could be reached precisely because they viewed the Italian state to be exceptionally weak and vulnerable. Yet most of the terrorists who held this view are now in prison or exile. What explains their misjudgment?

The Legal Context and the Initial Reactions

To evaluate the measures taken by the Italian state to combat terrorism we will begin by examining the legal and organizational environment that existed towards the end of the 1960s, that is the years immediately before the Piazza Fontana bank bombing and the advent of the era of terrorism. First, we will consider the status of the legal sanctions that could be used to combat terrorism, and then the organizations available to the authorities to apply these sanctions.

The Italian Constitution of 1947 is a document that asserts the principles of political and personal freedom commonly identified with liberal democracy. Its first section proclaims, *inter alia*, the freedoms of speech, press, association and assembly. The Constitution refers to the privacy of personal correspondence, the inviolability of domicile and the individual's right to move freely within Italy and to travel abroad. The document also prohibits capital punishment, except in wartime, ex post facto punishments and other measures incompatible with liberal democratic protections.[1] Despite the fact some of these provisions are qualified by references to their regulation by specific legislative enactments or judicial rulings, they represent the clear intent of their drafters to erase all traces of Fascism from the country's public life.

Two factors relevant to the terrorist experience need to be mentioned here. First, in 1947, the desire to eliminate Fascism was so great that members of the Constituent Assembly added a "transitional" provision (Number XII) to the Constitution that prohibited the reorganization of the previously dissolved Fascist party, "under any form whatsoever." Thus, the right of political association was not extended to those who wished to exercise it in order to achieve a Fascist revival. This restriction was not self-enforcing, however, subsidiary legislation was necessary to put it into practice. Also, the Constitution did not define Fascism.

Thus, despite the constitutional restriction, the neo-Fascist Italian Social movement (MSI) was organized and permitted to hold public rallies and participate in election campaigns. The Movement's anti-Communism, coupled with the Cold War atmosphere of the late 1940s, contributed to the government's decision to overlook these developments.[2] However, in 1982, after the MSI had achieved a significant electoral success in the South, largely at the Christian Democrats' expense, and after a number of widely publicized acts of "neo-squadrism", Parliament passed the Scelba Law (N. 645 of June 20, 1952 and named after Interior Minister Mario Scelba) that was intended to implement the constitutional prohibition on Fascist activity. Although the measure did not mention the MSI by name, it did, after a fashion, define Fascist activity. Any group or association of five or more persons which advocated the use of violence for political ends, proposed the suppression of freedoms guaranteed under the Constitution, denigrated the values of democracy and the wartime resistance, and promoted racist propaganda, fell within the meaning of the term "Fascism". Penal sanctions were imposed on the organizers and members of such a Fascist group or association. Further, whenever, as a result of an investigation and trial, a court determined that a particular group or association met these standards, the minister of interior was then authorized to dissolve it.[3]

The subsequent reluctance of the judicial authorities and the government to enforce the law during the 1950s and 60s became a matter of controversy. The MSI was not dissolved, but persisted as a parliamentary party; nor were prosecutions undertaken to eliminate the New Order and National Vanguard formations, despite their more open avowals of the values and practices defined as Fascist under the law. Occasionally, individuals caught while engaging in acts of neo-Fascist violence were also prosecuted for violations of the Scelba law, but the neo-Fascist organizations themselves were left intact.[4] By the late 1960s, the Italian left and the Communists especially held the justifiable view that the government was unwilling to proscribe neo-Fascism, that is, was willing to look the other way and thereby tacitly condone neo-Fascist activities.[5] Nevertheless, we should keep in mind the fact that in 1969, at the beginning of the terrorist experience, there already existed legislation which at least in theory could be used to deal with its right-wing perpetrators.

While the first section of the Constitution was intended to protect the freedom of political association and other liberal democratic rights, the same cannot be said for the country's penal codes. In particular, the criminal and criminal procedure codes were documents that had been drafted and put into effect during the Fascist era. Accordingly, many of their provisions seem incompatible with the principles expressed in the Constitution. Despite this fact, the codes were left in force long after the Constitution went into effect.[6] Thus, in the same way those in political power were reluctant to apply the Scelba law and conform to constitutional intention, so too, they were slow to modify Italy's Fascist era legal codes.

The Criminal Code not only contains standard provisions covering such crimes as murder, kidnapping, robbery, etc., all pertinent to terrorist behavior, but many of its articles embody the Fascist-based notion of the political crime. Of particular relevance are the provisions dealing with conspiracies and attacks aimed at overthrowing the state. Article 270 seeks to penalize the organizers and members of "subversive associations." The latter are defined as groups whose aims are the establishment, through violence, of a dictatorship of one social class over another.[7] This measure, clearly directed at Marxist-Leninist groups, was still in effect in 1969. Also available to the authorities in that year was Article 306 (and several adjacent articles) which imposes penal sanctions on individuals who form, promote or join an "armed band" whose purpose is the violent overthrow of the Italian state.

While Articles 270 and 306 criminalize association or membership in violent or allegedly violent political groups, other articles protect the state against overt behavior. Thus, the Code (articles 283 and 284) refers to the crimes of the armed insurrection against and violent attacks on the state.[8]

Armed with this array of criminal laws, it is not surprising that Italian legislators did not react immediately to the onset of terrorism by enacting a wholly new set of emergency measures to meet this new threat. Apparently, the state already had what it needed to fight it. What may have been missing was an accurate appraisal of the threat or a willingness to enforce the law.

We must also take into consideration here the status of the criminal procedure code. In the period 1968–72 and as the result of rulings by Italy's constitutional court and new legislation, this code was liberalized so as to better protect the rights of individuals suspected or accused of criminal activity.[9] Thus, at precisely the time terrorism was emerging as a significant factor in public life, suspects were obtaining, for example, the right to remain silent when confronted by police interrogation, and the right to have a defense lawyer present at an early stage of the judicial process. Of course, these were sensible reforms aimed at bringing the code into conformity with the spirit of the constitution, but their timing was decidedly inauspicious.

The ability of a state to combat terrorism is dependent not only on what the laws says, but on the capacities of the organizations responsible for its enforcement. On paper, the situation as of the late 1960s was not especially bleak, so far as the defense of the democratic order is concerned.

The state police apparatus was able to furnish the interior ministry with a long list of potential terrorists by December 1970. The police had special "political" offices in each of its provincial headquarters and the Carabinieri, the other major national police force, had a special brigade with the responsibility to deal with public order and civil disturbances.[10] The major problem concerned Italy's intelligence service. As we have noted earlier, SIFAR (the Servizio informazioni forze armate) had been the object of accusation and a source of scandal during the mid-1960s. As a result of the De Lorenzo Affair, the organization had been reformed and renamed as the Defense Information Service (SID) in 1965–66. Like its predecessor, SID was subordinate to the defense ministry. Section "D" of SID had responsibility for domestic counterespionage operations. To this end, it was divided into 23 territorial units, each of which was headed by an officer of the Carabinieri.

The problem was not that of organizational format, but of the political orientation of Section "D's" personnel. As subsequent events were to reveal, a number of these personnel, including some at the highest levels, were sympathetic to the neo-Fascist groups which were committed to subverting Italian democracy. As this became clear, in connection with the investigation of the Piazza Fontana bombing, there were new calls for reform and reorganization. It is of course, no small thing to say that one of the agencies responsible for detecting terrorist activities was itself populated by individuals associated with neo-Fascist organizations embarked on a violent project to undermine the democratic order. Yet in the early years of terrorism, SID was more a part of the problem than its solution.

*   *   *

If the foregoing was the situation that existed as the terrorist experience began, let us now turn our attention to the ways in which the Italian state responded to that experience. As with our earlier discussion, so too here; it is important to bear in mind that the terrorist experience is divisible into two episodes: the first dating from 1969 and continuing until the mid-1970s; and the second beginning in 1976–77 and ending in 1982–83. It should also be recalled that terrorism during the first episode was dominated by the neo-Fascists while terrorism during the second was largely a leftist phenomenon. Furthermore, if we judge the severity of the threat by the number of attacks perpetrated by the terrorists, the second period was also the time of maximum stress on the state.

In both periods, events dictated the state's response. Since the neo-Fascists posed the greatest danger during the first, the legislative and organizational response was focused primarily on responding to the rightist danger.

From an organizational perspective, the government reacted to the neo-Fascist caused *Italicus* train derailment and Piazza La Loggia bombing, as well as the Red Brigades' kidnapping of state prosecutor Mario Sossi, all occurring in 1974, by creating two bodies. Under pressure from the press and public, the Christian Democratic government of Prime Minister Mariano Rumor formed the General Inspectorate against Terrorism and Armed Bands.[11] Emilio Santillo, a former police chief in Turin and Reggio Calabria, was designated to lead this nationwide organization and report on its work to the head of the state police. According to rumor, the Inspectorate was principally responsible for combating neo-Fascist violence. Also in 1974, a special anti-terrorism unit of the police in Turin was created and placed under the direction of Carabinieri General Carlo Alberto dalla Chiesa.[12] It was assigned the task of countering the Red Brigades.

The legislative measures Parliament adopted during the first half of the 1970s to cope with the threat do not make specific reference to terrorism. Nevertheless, they were intended to stiffen the penalties and to strengthen the hands of the police against persons engaged in this endeavor.

Legislation was enacted in 1974 lengthening the sentences of those found guilty of illegally possessing arms and munitions and for those caught while seeking to smuggle these implements into Italy.[13] But the major piece of anti-terrorist legislation in this period was the Reale (after the Justice Minister Oronzo Reale Public Order Law [N. 152 of 22 May, 1975]). Justified by the government as a mechanism necessary to defeat neo-Fascist violence, the act, among other things, amended and strengthened the 1952 Scelba law by extending the prison terms of those convicted for Fascist activities and by permitting the government to dissolve Fascist organizations in emergency situations without the requirement of a prior judicial finding. In addition to its specifically anti-Fascist component the Reale law also contained more general provision concerning sanctions against political violence. Article 1 required mandatory confinement (or denied "provisional liberty") for those charged but not yet tried with having committed murder, attacks on the president of the republic and the constitution, armed insurrection against the state, forming or joining an "armed band", the illegal possession or manufacture of weapons and a number of other violent acts (e.g., derailing trains) included in the terrorist repetoire. Procedurally, the Reale law aided the police by making it easier for them to detain, question and search suspects and by liberalizing the conditions under which they might draw their weapons for these purposes.[14]

The latter provisions were strongly criticized by Radical party deputies on civil libertarian grounds. Losing their case in Parliament, the Radicals subsequently gathered sufficient signatures on a public petition to have a national referendum held in an attempt to have the law abrogated. But when the referendum was finally held in June 1978, after the kidnaping and murder of Aldo Moro, the electorate voted by a substantial margin to retain the measure.

Analysts of Italian politics, particularly those on the left, were extremely critical of the government's performance in combating neo-Fascist terrorism in this period. The obvious grounds for these criticisms were the investigations and prosecutions of those neo-Fascists apparently responsible for the Piazza Fontana, Italicus and Piazza La Loggia massacres. The evident involvement of some SID officers in right-wing terrorism served to amplify the accusations. The performance, though, does not seem to have been quite as bad as the government's opponents suggested.

While it is true that the prosecutions of those allegedly involved in these stragi were often mishandled, whether innocently or on purpose, the government's record was not totally one of failure and incompetence. By 1976, the New Order, National Vanguard, National Front and lesser neo-Fascist bands had been dissolved and most of their adherents arrested. The neo-Fascists' para-military training camps had been uncovered and their staffs arrested as were several police and military officers suspected of involvement in the various neo-Fascist insurrectionary schemes.

As will be recalled (see Chapter 2), the existence of the leftist revolutionary groups also appeared to have come to an end. The Red Brigades 'historic nucleus' was on trial, most members of the Nuclei of Armed Proletarians had been captured and the Partisan Action Groups, as well as the October 22 band, had been repressed before they could do much damage. Finally, because of the highly publicized accusations against some of its personnel, the operations of SID became subject to still another parliamentary investigation.

So it seemed by the middle of 1976 that despite its reputation for ineffectiveness, the state had successfully defeated the terrorist organizations on both the left and right. All this had been accomplished without any specific reference in the criminal law to the concept of terrorism.

The Decisive Measures

What was not anticipated was the dramatic revival of the phenomenon in 1976–77. Organizationally, the rapid escalation of terrorist violence did not occur at a propitious time. For reasons still not entirely clear, the government disbanded its special anti-terrorism units in 1976. The functions performed by the Santillo and Dalla Chiesa units were re-assigned to SID. The latter because of the suspicions aroused by its apparent involvement with the neo-Fascists, was, in turn, subject to reorganization. Rather like the Central Intelligence Agency in the United States in the aftermath of the Vietnam era, there was widespread feeling that the Italian service needed closer supervision by the legislature in order to achieve more accountability to democratic institutions.[15]

In response, the government of Giulio Andreotti introduced a bill in the fall of 1976 designed to reform the intelligence apparatus. After extensive hearings and debate, the reform law went into effect in October 1977 (N. 806 of October 24, 1977).[16] Among the principal changes adopted under the statute were these. First, the prime minister was made responsible for the overall supervision of intelligence and security policy. To assist him in this task, the law created two bodies. An interministerial committee representing concerned ministries (foreign affairs, interior defense, justice, industry and finance) was formed. Further, an executive committee for the intelligence and security services (CESIS) was organized to provide the prime minister with all information necessary to carry out this supervisory responsibility. Composed of the directors of the new intelligence and security services and other officials appointed by the prime minister, CESIS was also assigned the job of coordinating the work of these agencies. In addition, the law authorized the prime minister to create whatever special anti-terrorism organs he believed necessary.

In order to make the intelligence and security agencies more democratically accountable, the legislation required the government to send a written report to Parliament describing their activities every six months. It further empowered Parliament to form a joint committee of the Chamber of Deputies and Senate to monitor enforcement and conduct oversight investigations.

Importantly, the reform reorganized the scandal-ridden SID by dividing its functions and assigning them to two new bodies. The Service for Intelligence and Military Security (SISMI) was made responsible for military security, counterespionage and foreign intelligence gathering. SISMI became part of the defense ministry. The new agency responsible for domestic security and consequently the detection of domestic terrorist groups was named the Service for Intelligence and Democratic Security (SISDE). SISDE was placed under the supervision of the interior minister. The latter took an additional step to combat terrorism. In January 1978, the interior minister formed a Central Bureau for General Investigations and Special Operations (UCIGOS). Its principal task was to coordinate the operations of a newly created anti-terrorist field agency, the Division for General Investigations and Special Operations (DIGOS), of the state police force. With offices housed in the *questure* (police headquarters) of the country's regional capitals, the DIGOS were to play a leading role in the day-to-day struggle against the terrorist groups.

The major problem with the reforms of the intelligence and police functions just described was not with the organizations they brought into being, although there was some confusion over their responsibilities. Nor did the problem have to do with the government's reluctance to take the terrorist threat seriously: far from it. Instead, the problem with these reforms concerned their timing. The kidnapping on March 16, 1978 of Aldo Moro and his murder by the Red Brigades 55 days later occurred just as the new anti-terrorism apparatus was being put in place. According to one parliamentary report on the event, at the time Moro was kidnapped SISDE consisted of fewer than 100 employees, most of whom held clerical and support positions.[17] Worse still, some of the suspect personnel from the dissolved Section "D" of SID had been transferred to posts in the new SISDE apparatus. And worst of all, the directors of the new intelligence organs, SISDE, SISMI and CESIS, were later discovered to have belonged to the secretive Masonic lodge *Propaganda Due*.[18] Although they resigned after the tragic conclusion of the Moro case, serious questions have been raised over their handling of the affair. Was the Moro case somehow manipulated or "instrumentalized" by them in such a way as to advance the lodge's political objectives? These objectives were unlikely to have included the "historic compromise" and the Communists' entry into Italy's ruling coalition or, in other words, precisely the task Moro was seeking to perform at the time he was taken captive by the Red Brigades. Could it be that the Red Brigades and the right-wing *Propaganda Due* shared an interest in sabotaging the "historic compromise"? These questions still remain to be answered.

The Moro case had several consequences with regard to the general issue of terrorism. Aside from replacing the heads of SISDE, SISMI and CESIS, the Andreotti government reacted by placing Carabinieri General Dalla Chiesa at the head of a special anti-terrorism unit with the specific responsibility of defeating the Red Brigades. Later to be assassinated by the mafia in Sicily, at the time of his appointment, Dalla Chiesa was a man of

58, from Piedmont, who had earlier succeeded in destroying the Red Brigades' "historic nucleus" by having one of his agents infiltrate the organization. Working from a carefully guarded office located in the middle of a Carabinieri base outside of Rome, Dalla Chiesa began his effort to repress the Red Brigades in the summer of 1978.[19]

There were other indications of the seriousness with which the government regarded the growing threat of left-wing terrorism. New maximum security prisons were to be built in order to prevent the escape of captured terrorists, escapes that had occurred with some frequency in the past. Further, both the state police and the Carabinieri, the two major national police forces, organized special intervention teams of officers prepared to assault terrorist bases and hideouts. Modeled after their counterparts in West Germany and Great Britain, one of these teams (known as "leatherheads", *teste di cuoio*) would later be used to liberate American General James Dozier from his Red Brigades captors in 1982.[20]

Until Moro's abduction Italian criminal law had contained no specific reference to the concept of terrorism. But this was to change. Within a week of the kidnapping, the government issued a decree having the force of law which was later modified and formally adopted by Parliament to become Law N. 191 of May 18, 1978.[21] Titled Penal and Procedural Norms for the Prevention and Repression of Grave Crimes, the act established the crime of "terrorism or subversion of the democratic order" and changed both the criminal and criminal procedure codes to take account of the concept. The criminal code was amended (Article 289) to include the crime of kidnapping for purposes of terrorism and subverting the democratic order. Those found guilty of this crime were to be sentenced to prison terms ranging from 25 to 30 years. And if the victim was killed by his/her captors, those responsible were to be given life imprisonment with no possibility of parole. Importantly, though, the law offered reduced sentences of 2 to 4 years for those terrorist kidnappers who disassociated themselves from other members of their group and helped the authorities locate and free the hostage. Although this carrot and stick measure did not produce results in the Moro case, it represented a significant first step in the application of a tactic that would be used by the authorities to dismantle the terrorist organizations.

In addition to the introduction of this new terrorist crime, the 1978 legislation modified the criminal procedure code and related laws in ways that aided the investigation of terrorist groups. As will be recalled, the criminal procedure laws had been liberalized during the 1968–72 period so as to better protect the rights of citizens asserted in the Italian Constitution. The terrorist threat and the state's reaction to it reversed this trend. Thus, it became easier, with the enactment of the 1978 law, for the authorities to tap telephones in what were defined as emergency situations. The police acquired the ability to detain any person who refused to identify himself or herself and to question without the presence of an attorney those caught while committing a crime. Finally, because the terrorist groups frequently rented homes or apartments, using assumed names, for use as hideouts, the law required landlords or property owners to notify the police within 48 hours of new renters or buyers of their property. The new occupants would then be subject to police investigations.

The 1978 law and the various anti-terrorist organizations put in place by the government began to have some effect, yet they hardly brought an end to terrorist activity. Accordingly, after the 1979 parliamentary elections, the first held after Moro's assassination and after the highly publicized arrest of Professor Antonio Negri for allegedly masterminding the entire revolutionary enterprise, the government issued a decree (N. 625 of December 15, 1979) which was then intensely debated in Parliament before its conversion into law in February 1980 (Law N. 15 of February 6, 1980) as Urgent Measures for The Protection of The Democratic Order and Public Security.[22] Substantively, the scope of this law was considerably wider than its predecessor. Two new crimes were created. Article 270 of the criminal code (on subversive association) was amended to make it a crime for individuals to join, promote, constitute, organize or direct an association that sought to subvert the democratic order by violent means. Prison terms ranging from 4 to 15 years were provided for those found guilty of this crime. And still longer sentences were to be imposed on those found guilty of committing violent crimes for terrorist or subversive ends (Article 280 of the criminal code).

Parliamentary debate over the need to establish these new crimes, conducted in the wake of the Negri arrest, was particularly heated. Senators representing the Radical and Republican parties voiced their opposition based on civil libertarian considerations. The opponents argued that terms like "terrorist or subversive ends" were excessively vague and ambiguous. The government, they maintained, was seeking to make belief or ideology into a crime. One legislator contended that the already existing provisions in the criminal code covering membership in subversive associations and armed bands had been sufficient for the Fascist regime to repress its opponents, were not these same measures adequate now? Was it necessary for the democratic regime to adopt new instruments of repression that embellished those used by Mussolini's regime?[23] These objections were overridden and the decree was converted into law. However, the Radicals, just as they had done in the case of the Reale law, succeeded in gaining enough signatures on a public petition to have its abrogation considered by the electorate at a referendum. But again, as with the Reale law, so too on this occasion; a majority of Italian voters chose to uphold the legislation at a 1981 referendum.

Another section of the 1980 law stimulated less debate but proved to be more important than the above in bringing about the terrorist groups' elimination. This provision (covered by Articles 4 and 5) offered radically reduced prison terms for those found guilty of belonging to a terrorist group or committing violent crimes for terrorist or subversive ends if they were willing to disassociate themselves from their colleagues and furnish help to the authorities. "Repentant" (pentiti) terrorists who were willing to renounce their lives of violence, identify other members of their group, and provide the authorities with other forms of concrete assistance had their sentences diminished.

The law contained additional provisions which, inter alia, made it easier for the police to arrest suspected terrorists and conduct warrant-free searches of whole neighborhoods in which they were thought to be hiding. But it was the extension of leniency in return for disassociation that had the greatest impact.

Patrizio Peci, then a member of the Red Brigades' Strategic Direction, reports being in a condition of personal crisis during this period. Disenchanted with the Red Brigades and its prospects, he felt tired of the struggle and profoundly stressed by the need to live the clandestine life of a wanted terrorist.[24] Instead of excitement, he had found a life that was for the most part, boring, and one passed largely without female companionship. Other terrorists were experiencing feelings of remorse over the uselessness of the violence at this time. One member of Front Line told an investigator: "I think the moment of my arrest was the most liberating of my entire life."[25]

Feelings such as these, evidently, were widely diffused in terrorist circles. When they were caught by the DIGOS or Dalla Chiesa's agents some felt a genuine need to explain themselves and confess. And after his arrest, Peci, at least, reports being surprised by his feelings towards his captors.

The so-called 'Stockholm Syndrome' has been the subject of substantial commentary in the literature on terrorism. This 'syndrome' refers to the inclination of some victims taken captive by terrorist groups to develop sympathetic feelings towards their captors and their political goals. In Peci's case, there was apparently a reversal of the phenomenon. After his arrest, this revolutionary enemy of the Italian state reported developing a sense of identification with the officers who held him in custody. As he perceived them, they turned out to be young and thoughtful men, such as he saw himself, not the sadists he had expected or imagined them to be.

If we couple the mental conditions of many terrorists in 1980 with the now legally sanctioned possibility of returning to a normal life after a relatively brief prison term, their willingness to disassociate and repent is not hard to explain. Perhaps their willingness to inform on their fellow revolutionaries was not exactly an exhibition of personal heroism, but it was nonetheless, an entirely human reaction under the circumstances.

The 1980 law granting reduced sentences to those who disassociated themselves from the terrorist organizations and then provided help to the authorities yielded a bonanza of arrests. As one terrorist was captured he/ she furnished the authorities with the names of other terrorists. In turn, when the latter were arrested, several of their number repented and offered still more names, etc. It was through this process that the police were able to learn the whereabouts of General Dozier and then free him from his Red Brigades' kidnappers in January 1982.

Following Dozier's liberation, the 1980 legislation was widely viewed as so successful that Parliament passed another law (N. 304 of May 29, 1982) that refined and liberalized its provisions on disassociation. This measure extended clemency, no punishment, to those guilty of membership in terrorist groups, armed bands or subversive associations, if they were willing to repent and provide the authorities with help. And, in addition, it offered reduced prison terms for repentant terrorists responsible for acts of violence. Finally, this legislation imposed a deadline of January 29, 1983 after which the rewards for repentance would revert to those provided under the 1980 law.[26]

By January 29, 1983, a total of 389 terrorists had taken advantage of the law and repented.[27] Their assistance, along with the anti-terrorism apparatus put in place after the Moro assassination, brought an end to Italy's second episode of terrorist violence. The measures on disassociation and repentance were not without their critics, however. Some have attacked this policy on the basis of inequity; two terrorists, one of whom has repented, will be given very different prison sentences for having committed the same acts of violence.[28] Others have argued that in their zeal to confess and save their own skins, the repentants have named individuals whose involvement with the terrorist groups was marginal at best. For example, the sister of a terrorist who provided her brother and his companions with a room in which to stay overnight is identified, charged, jailed and denied "provisional liberty" while she awaits trial for her "crime." Unable to repent because she does not have anything about which to repent, she is compelled to spend months or even years in prison. The critics certainly have a point. Instances of injustice, though disturbing, were probably inevitable in the defeat the state inflicted on terrorism.

The Lessons

This defeat was achieved without the imposition of martial law, although interestingly, the MSI's parliamentary leadership had advocated it, the use of torture to obtain information or, more generally, the interruption of the democratic political process. Further, it was accomplished despite the existence of significant disagreements among the country's political parties over who the terrorists were and how best to repress their organizations. The performance of the various state institutions given the responsibility for stopping the terrorists was far from perfect. As we have seen, these institutions were formed, dissolved and reorganized too frequently, a result, in part, of misjudgments about the dimensions of the problem with which they were confronted. To make matters worse, the terrorists' defeat was probably delayed by the evident collusion during the first wave of violence of security officers with the neo-Fascist groups.

Yet, despite these deficiencies, terrorism was defeated. What lessons may be drawn from this victory?

Part of the credit must go to the terrorists themselves. As organizations, the leftist groups became progressively more isolated from the working class constituency on whose behalf they sought to foment revolution. And when treated as individuals, when the terrorists were offered the opportunity to repent or disassociate, they were prepared to betray their comrades in exchange for a return to a normal life.

From the point of view of public policy, several measures appear to have been decisive. First, the recognition by policy-makers of terrorism as a serious threat, the neo-Fascist variety after the *stragi* of 1974 and the leftist one in 1978 after the Moro killing, led them to establish organizations capable of meeting the challenge it posed. Second, modifications in the laws governing criminal procedure made it easier for the police and judicial authorities to carry out their anti-terrorist tasks. These measures, though, had the unfortunate effect of reversing the trend towards extending the procedural rights of citizens that had begun just prior to the advent of the terrorist era. But now that terrorism has subsided, law makers are free to resume the reforms the terrorists induced them to abandon.

Third, the laws of 1980 and 1982 had the effect of simultaneously making it harder for individuals to continue as terrorists while making it easier for them to abandon their violent careers. Prison terms for terrorist acts and involvements were lengthened considerably, while those who disassociated and repented could envision a return to normal lives; this occurred in an environment in which the authorities, using improved techniques, had raised the probabilities that the terrorists would be apprehended. This strategy is one that policy-makers in other nations confronted by terrorist threats might well study with benefit.

On the other hand, sections of the 1980 law which criminalized membership or leadership of terrorist groups seem rather redundant. Since the criminal code already contained provisions on subversive associations, armed bands and the formation of Fascist groups, these additional criminal categories do not seem to have been warranted. Since the terrorist groups could (and often were) identified for legal purposes as falling under one or even all of the above proscribed organizations, the new designation may have had more to do with mollifying a disturbed public than eliminating the source of its fears.

Notes

1. For an English translation of the constitution see Norman Kogan, *The Government of Italy* (New York: Thomas Crowell, 1962) pp. 188–215.

2. Leonard Weinberg, *After Mussolini* (Washington, D.C.: University Press of America, 1979) pp. 22–23.

3. Mario Abate (ed.), *Il codice delle leggi di pubblica sicurezza* (Piacenza: La Tribuna, 1983) pp. 115–116.

4. Thus, Interior Minister Restivo reported to Parliament that 36 individuals were accused of having violated the law in 1967 and 15 in 1968; *Atti Parlamentari* V Legislatura, Senato della Repubblica, Seduta 416 (February, 1971) pp. 20, 571–20, 575.

5. See for example Pietro Secchia, *Lotta antifascista e giovani generazioni* (Milan: La Pietra, 1973) pp. 37–59.

6. Ettore Gallo and Enzo Musco, *Delitti contro l'ordine costituzione* (Bologna: Patron, 1984) pp. 20–21.

7. Dalberto Cassone and Renato Bricchetti (eds.), *Codici Penale e Di Procedura Penale* (Milan: Tramontana, 1983) p. 184.

8. *Ibid*, p. 187.

9. Vittorio Grevi, "Sistema penale dell'emergenza: la risposta legislativa al terrorismo," in Gianfranco Pasquino (ed.), *La prova delle armi* (Bologna: Il Mulino, 1984) pp. 17–20; see also Domenico Bartoli, *Nella terra di nessuno* (Milan: Mondadori, 1976) pp. 55–57.

10. Vittofranco Pisano, *A Study of The Restructured Italian Intelligence and Security Services* (Washington, D.C.: Library of Congress, 1978) pp. 68–69.

11. *La Stampa* (May 31, 1974) pp. 1–2.

12. Stefano Rodota, "La Risposta dello stato al terrorismo," in Pasquino (ed.), *op. cit.*, p. 86.

13. Grevi, *op. cit.*, pp. 20–24.

14. For the Reale law see Abate (ed.), *op. cit.*, pp. 141–145, and for a commentary, see Grevi, *op. cit.*, pp. 24–28.

15. *La Repubblica* (August 12, 1976) p. 3.

16. For an English language translation of the law see Pisano, *op. cit.*, pp. 35–49. For an account of the new police organs, see *Terrorism and Security: The Italian Experience*, Report of the Subcommittee on Security and Terrorism of the Committee on the Judiciary, United States Senate (Washington, D.C.: U.S. Government Printing Office, 1984) pp. 53, 54.

17. See the report of the Socialist members of the parliamentary committee on the Moro case, *Relazioni di Minoranza*, Commissione Parlamentare sulla Strage di Via Fani (Rome: Tipografia del Senato, 1983) p. 21.

18. See the majority report of the parliamentary committee on the Moro case, *Relazione della Commissione Parlamentare D'Inchiesta sulla Strage di Via Fani* (Rome: Tipografia del Senato, 1983) p. 56.

19. *La Repubblica* (August 11, 1978) p. 1.

20. *La Stampa* (January 29, 1982) p. 1.

21. For the text see Abate (ed.) *op. cit.*, pp. 146–147; for a commentary see Grevi, *op. cit.*, pp. 34–39.

22. For the text see Abate (ed.) *op. cit.*, pp. 147–148; for a commentary see Pier Luigi Vigna, *La Finalita di terrorisma ed eversione* (Varese: Giuffre Editore, 1981) pp. 21–83; and Gabriele Chelazzi, *La Disassociazione dal terrorismo* (Varese: Giuffre Editore, 1981) pp. 5–53.

23. Quoted in Vigna, *op. cit.*, pp. 127–128.

24. Giordano Bruno Guerri, *Patrizio Peci: Io L'Infame* (Milan: Mondadori, 1983) pp. 173–177.

25. Quoted in Luciana Stortoni, *Analisi di una organizzazione terrorista: Prima Linea*, tesi di laurea (Florence: Universita degli studi, Facolta di scienze politiche, 1983) p. 329.

26. For the 1982 text see Abate (ed.), *op. cit.*, pp. 149–151; for a commentary see Maurizio Laudi, *I Casi di non punibilita dei terroristi "pentiti"* (Varese: Giuffre Editore, 1983) pp. 11–148.

27. *La Repubblica* (January 29, 1983) p. 13.

28. Luigi De Ruggiero, "I problemi dai processi di terrorismo" in *La Magistratura di fronte al terrorismo e all'eversione di sinistra* (Milan: Franco Angelli Editore, 1982) pp. 29–36.

8
CONCLUSIONS

Domestic terrorism in Italy ended with a series of mass trials. In most of the cities that had been the sites of terrorist violence—Rome, Turin, Milan, Bologna, Florence, Padua—groups of handcuffed defendants were taken from prison and led into courtrooms where they were placed in large cages, rather like exotic animals in a zoo. There they sat or stood and listened to the charges brought against them. Nineteen eighty-three and the following year was the season for these trials.[1] Some of the defendants appeared defiant in the face of bourgeois justice; others seemed lethargic; a few exhibited contrition. Most of those who had refused to disassociate and repent had their lives ruined by their terrorist adventures. In general, the wheel of justice ground unevenly; the prosecutions against the leftists were more successful than those directed at the neo-Fascists.

Aside from the effect on those immediately involved, the terrorists and their victims, what impact has terrorism had on Italian politics? What lessons may be learned from the entire experience?

First, the experience itself was in part a legacy of the Italian past. Terrorists on both the left and right were captivated by ideas and events—a revolutionary working class, the Resistance, the march on Rome—that belonged to an earlier era of Italian history. One of the legacies bequeathed by the past to those who became terrorists was a profound suspicion concerning the actions and intentions of their opponents. Left and right came to see each other as depersonalized enemies to whom motivation was assigned by myths and ideologically filtered historical events.[2] Feltrinelli believed a Fascist coup d'etat was at hand and reacted by trying to create an armed opposition to it. Neo-Fascist leaders believed that a Communist conspiracy was at work and responded by devising a violent scheme of their own to thwart the Red's plan of subversion. The result of this process was a self-fulfilling prophecy or prophesies, in which each side acted as if the other posed a mortal danger to its basic political values.

This process seems to have been symptomatic of a highly polarized political order, with mass political parties and related organizations located at its extremes unreconciled to the existing system. Indeed, Sartori and other observers of Italian party politics during the 1950s and 60s described it as one of "polarized pluralism."[3] Examining the same era, Dahl refers to the tendency of the Italian system to develop oppositions based on deductive, abstract principles rather than empirical criteria.[4] Deducing the nature of one's political opponents from historically and ideologically derived categories, of course, facilitates their depersonalization. When the "enemy" is not a person but a category the resort to violence is made easier.

While the terrorists may have operated on the basis of these polarized and deductive conceptions, the political system as a whole was moving in the opposite direction. During the 1970s and 80s it has seemingly become less polarized. The Communist party no longer represents an opposition in principle to the constitutional system. On the right, the Italian Social Movement (MSI) has resumed the relatively conservative role it played in practice before the era of conflict began. It is interesting to note here that when Communist party secretary Enrico Berlinguer died in 1984, one of the political figures who paid his condolences at PCI headquarters in Rome was Giorgio Almirante, the MSI leader. Quite inadvertently, the terrorists may have contributed to the consolidation and depolarization of Italian democracy. What brought about this obviously paradoxical result? How could terrorist violence aimed at destabilizing and eventually toppling Italy's democratic regime have promoted the opposite consequence?

To begin, we should bear in mind that Italian terrorists initiated their violent activities with a relatively realistic appraisal of their country's political condition. In the years leading up to the violence, not only the future terrorists but also academic social scientists observed repeatedly that alienation and disenchantment were sentiments widely distributed and strongly felt by Italians when they evaluated their country's democracy. It was a regime widely perceived as ineffective, corrupt and immobile, one which elicited little enthusiasm from most of those it sought to govern.[5] In this regard, the Italian condition was very much unlike circumstances prevailing in the United States, West Germany or Japan. In these nations it required that potential terrorists possess imaginations rich enough for them to believe their meager bands might somehow threaten the existing order. In the Italian case, it did not require all that great a distortion of reality to conclude that a violent change in regime was a realistic possibility, one which might evoke massive popular support.

Why then, to repeat, did the terrorists inadvertently promote the consolidation of the regime they held in such contempt? Part of the answer may be found in the behavior of the country's political parties and the reactions they elicited from the electorate.

TABLE 8.1
Support for the MSI and PCI at National Elections of 1968,1972,1976
and 1979 (Per Cent of Popular Vote)

	1968	1972	1976	1979
MSI	4.5	8.7	6.1	5.3
PCI	27.0	27.2	34.4	30.4

Source: Howard Penniman (ed.), Italy at the Polls: The Parliamentary
Elections of 1976 (Washington, D.C.: American Enterprise Institute,1977)
pp. 356-371; Howard Penniman (ed.), Italy at the Polls, 1979 (Washington,
D.C.: American Enterprise Institute, 1981) pp.312-323.

In writing about the relationship between political violence and the breakdown of democratic regimes, Juan Linz assigns particular importance to the response of government bodies and major political parties to the violence.[6] In cases where these institutions do not recognize the violent groups as legitimate political actors, the latter's chances of success are diminished, the prospects for a breakdown reduced.

This was by and large the case in Italy. We should pay particular attention to those political parties,the MSI and PCI, that prompted Sartori, Dahl and others to describe Italy in the 1950s and 60s as a polarized system with parties at the Right and Left ends of the ideological spectrum opposed in principle to the constitutional order.

The generalization is that these parties were rewarded when they were perceived in the electorate and elsewhere as opposed to political violence and punished when they were viewed however dimly as somehow linked to terrorism. At the 1972 parliamentary elections (see Table 8.1) the MSI campaigned as a party committed to a restoration of law and order in a strife torn country. Its spokesman emphasized the MSI support for traditional symbols of authority: family, Church and nation. The election returns showed a dramatic surge in the party's support among Italian voters. However, between 1972 and 1976 there were a series of disclosures, widely reported by the mass media, of ties between the MSI, the neo-Fascist terrorist groups and various acts of political violence. Illustratively, during the 1976 election campaign one of the MSI's parliamentary candidates shot and killed a youthful protestor at a rally held on the outskirts of Rome. Events such as this contributed to a growing public perception that the MSI was contributing to the problem of terrorism rather than its solution. This view likely contributed to its decline at the polls in 1976.

The reward and punishment case for the Communists is admittedly more complicated. Nevertheless, despite the PCI's vigorous and uncompromising opposition to terrorism, the party suffered as the result of a growing public awareness, heightened by the 1978 Moro kidnapping and murder, that a good deal of the violence was caused by groups belonging to the same Marxist-Leninist tradition with which the PCI was identified. In municipal elections held on May 14, 1978, less than a week after Moro's body was discovered, the party's vote declined by more than 9 percent compared to the last elections held in the same localities.[7] And at the subsequent parliamentary elections in 1979, the PCI experienced its first significant national election decline since World War II. During the election campaign the Christian Democrats exploited the symbol of their martyred leader to portray themselves as the victims of terrorism while depicting the Communists as "slow in realizing the danger of terrorism, slow in recognizing the need for adequate defensive preparations."[8]

In neither the case of the MSI nor that of the PCI was the short-term waning of their electoral support brought about exclusively by popular perceptions that they had served as incubators of terrorists. Other forces were at work. Nonetheless, these perceptions, exploited by their opponents, did have some effect. If, instead, they had been rewarded by more votes rather than punished by less, would their public opposition to the terrorist groups have become muted, their outlook more accepting?

If the Italian public administered a kind of reward and punishment schedule to the political parties based on its perception of their relationship to terrorism, the question which needs to be answered is why the public, or an overwhelming majority of it, came to see terrorism in such a negative way? To answer it we need to turn our attention to the mass media's role in influencing the public reaction.

Naturally, the mass media were not all of one mind on the subject. Yet there were certain central tendencies in the way terrorist activities were portrayed in the press and on television. First, there was an initial tendency to view these activities, in the years immediately after Piazza Fontana, as exclusively Fascist in character. In light of the fact that Fascism, with its connotations of war and national degradation, is, to put it mildly, a highly negative symbol for massive segments of the public, it is no wonder that terrorism was perceived with hostility. But there are other media related explanations for this perception. Another is that the media repeatedly communicated vivid descriptions and pictures of terrorism's victims. These portrayals included not only accounts of political leaders, Aldo Moro most conspicuously, but of ordinary people who were killed or maimed as the result of terrorist atrocities. Thirdly, after the murder of prosecutor Coco in 1976 and particularly in their coverage of the Moro case, the mass media recognized that terrorist acts were being committed by groups with clear Marxist-Leninist credentials. Yet there was also an increasing tendency to depict their acts as ones of senseless bestiality, devoid of serious political content.[9]

Ironically the mass media's picture of terrorism was even made to fit the public's pre-existing perception of an ineffective and incompetent Italian government. Just as this government had been depicted on many occasions as incompetent in its handling of such natural or man-made catastrophies as earthquakes and cholera epidemics so too it was portrayed as ineffective in its struggle against terrorism. But the effect of this portrait hardly enhanced the terrorists' public support or political prospects. Instead, it stimulated public demands for more effective measures to repress their activities. The demands led to the removal of neo-Fascist well wishers in the military and police apparatus as well as the reorganization of both the police and security services and the spate of anti-terrorist legislation we have discussed.

* * *

One of the practical lessons from the sad experience of terrorism concerns the policy the Italian authorities applied to end it. Specifically, the strategy of strengthening the sanctions against persons who continued their involvements in terrorist groups while simultaneously making it easier for their members to disassociate themselves and resume normal lives seems to have been successful. The context, though, was one in which the authorities had created anti-terrorist units which had already begun to raise the probability that the terrorists would be caught. If this had not been true, it is unclear if the incentives offered for repentance would have had the same effect.

A more general lesson we may take from the Italian experience concerns the prospects for violent change in the industrialized democracies. Despite all the widely publicized flaws in Italian democracy, it proved, nonetheless, impervious to both the revolutionary designs of the leftists and the anti-constitutional schemes of the neo-Fascists. Although they may attract enormous publicity and cause some disruption, the terrorists cannot succeed in their ultimate aims. In Italy, they did not come close.

Notes

1. In terms of the large number of defendants at these trials and their confinement within barred enclosures in the courtroom, the anti-terrorist trials of 1982–83 bore considerable resemblance to the prosecutions against anarchists at the end of the 19th century. See Romano Canosa and Amadeo Santosuosso, *Magistrati, Anarchici E Socialisti* (Milan: Feltrinelli, 1981) pp. 89–105.

2. David Finlay, Ole Holsti and Richard Fagen, *Enemies in Politics* (Chicago: Rand McNally, 1967) pp. 1–24.

3. Giovanni Sartori, "European Political Parties: The Case of Polarized Pluralism," in Joseph LaPalombara and Myron Weiner (ed.), *Political Parties and Political Development* (Princeton: Princeton University Press, 1966) pp. 137–176.

4. Robert Dahl, *Political Opposition in Western Democracies* (New Haven: Yale University Press, 1966) pp. 353–355.

5. See for example, Joseph LaPaolombara, "Italy: Fragmentation, Isolation and Alienation," in Lucian Pye and Sidney Verba (eds.), *Political Culture and Political Development* (Princeton: Princeton University Press, 1965) pp. 282–329.

6. Juan Linz, *Crisis, Breakdown and Reequilibration* (Baltimore: The Johns Hopkins University Press, 1978) pp. 56–58.

7. Douglas Wertman, "The Christian Democrats: Masters of Survival," in Howard Penniman (ed.), *Italy at The Polls, 1979* (Washington, D.C.: American Enterprise Institute, 1981) p. 91.

8. *Ibid.* p. 96.

9. Carlo Marletti, "Terrorismo E Comunicazioni Di Massa," in Gianfranco Pasquino (ed.), *La Prova Delle Armi* (Bologna: Il Mulino, 1984) p. 151.

BIBLIOGRAPHY

Books

Abate, Mario (ed.) *Il codice delle leggi di pubblica sicurezza*. Piacenza: La Tribuna, 1983.

Acquaviva, Sabino. *Il seme religioso della rivolta*. Milan: Rizzoli editore, 1979.

_____. *Guerriglia e guerra rivoluziolnaria in Italia*. Milan: Rizzoli editors, 1979.

Almirante, Giorgio. *La Strategia del terrorismo*. Rome: SAIPEM: 1974.

Barbieri, Daniele. *Agenda nera: trent'anni di neofascismo in Italia*. Rome: Coines edizioni, 1976.

Bartoli, Domenico. *Nella Terra di nessuno*. Milan: Mondadori, 1976.

Bechelloni, Giovanni. *Cultura e ideologia nella nuova sinistra*. Milan: Communita, 1973.

Becker, Jillian. *Hilter's Children*. New York: J.P. Lippincott, 1977.

Bobbio, Luigi. *Lotta continua*. Rome: Savelli, 1979.

Bocca, Giorgio. *Il terrorismo italiano*. Milan: Rizzoli editore, 1978.

Bocca, Giorgio (ed.) *Moro: una tragedia italiana*. Milan: Bompiani, 1978.

_____. *Storia dell Italia partigiana*. Bari: Laterza, 1977.

Bonante, Luigi (ed.) *Dimensioni del terrorismo politico*. Milan: Angelli editore, 1979.

Cancogni, Manlio. *Gli squadristi*. Milan: Longanesi & Co., 1980.

Canosa, Romano and Santosuosso, Amadeo. *Magistrati, Anarchici e socialisti*. Milan: Feltrinelli, 1981.

Cassone, Dalberto and Bricchetti, Renato (eds.) *Codici penali e di procedura penale*. Milan: Tramontana, 1983.

Castellano, Lucio (ed.) *Aut Op: la storia e i documenti da potere operaio all'autonomia organizzata*. Milan: Savelli, 1980.

Chelazzi, Gabriele. *La disassociazione dal terrorismo*. Varese: Giuffre Editore, 1981.

Chiarini, Roberto and Corsini, Paolo. *Da Salo a Piazza Della Loggia*. Milan: Franco Angelli, 1983.

Coi, Andrea, Galliani, Prospero, Piccioni, Francesco and Seghetti, Bruno. *Politica e rivoluzione*. Milan: Giuseppe Mai, 1983.

_____. *Italia 1983: prigioneri, processi, progetti*. Rome: Cooperativa Apache, 1983.

Coletti, Alessandro. *Anarchici e questori*. Padova: Marsilio editore, 1971.

D'Agostini, Fabrizio. *Reggio Calabria*. Milan: Feltrinelli, 1972.

141

Dahl, Robert. *Political Opposition in Western Democracies*. New Haven: Yale University Press, 1966.

De Felice, Renzo. *Mussolini il fascista: la conquista del potere, 1921–1925*. Turin: Einaudi Editore, 1966.

Della Porta, Donatella. "Le cause del terrorismo nelle societa contemporanee." Donatella della Porta and Gianfranco Pasquino (eds.) *Terrorismo e violenza politica*. Bologna: Il Mulino, 1983.

—————. *I terrorismi in Italia tra il 1969 e il 1982*. Bologna: Cattaneo, 1983.

—————, and Maurizio Rossi. *Cifre crudelli: bilancio dei terrorismi italiani*. Bologna: Cattaneo, 1984.

—————. *I terrorismi in Italia tra il 1969 e il 1982*. Bologna: Cattaneo, 1983.

Delzell, Charles. *Mussolini's Enemies*. Princeton, N.J.: Princeton University Press, 1961.

De Ruggiero, Luigi. *La Magistratura di fronte al terrorismo ed all' eversione di sinistra*. Milan: Franco Angelli editore, 1982.

De Simone, Cesare. *La Pista Nera*. Rome: Riuniti, 1972.

Ferraresi, Franco (ed.) *La destra radicale*. Milan: Feltrinelli, 1984.

Ferrarotti, Franco. *Fascismo di ritorno*. Rome: Edizioni delle lega per le autonomie e i poteri locali, 1975.

—————. *L ipnosi della violenza*. Milan: Rizzoli editore, 1980.

Finetti, Ugo. *Il dissenso nel PCI*. Milan: Sugar edizioni, 1978.

Fini, Marco and Barberi, Andrea. *Valpreda: processo al processo*. Milan: Feltrinelli, 1974.

Finlay, David, Holsti, Ole, and Fagen, Richard. *Enemies in Politics*. Chicago: Rand McNally, 1976.

Freda, Giorgia. *La disintegrazione del sistema*. Padua: Edizioni AR, 1969.

Gaddi, Giuseppe. *Neofascismo in Europa*. Milan: la Pietra, 1974.

Galleni, Mauro (ed.) *Rapporto sul terrorismo*. Milan: Rizzoli Editore, 1981.

Galli, Giorgio. "La componente magica della cultura di destra." Guido Quazza (ed.) *Fascismo oggi: nuova destra e cultura reazionaria negli anni ottanta*. Cuneo: Istituto Storico della Resistenza, 1983.

Gallo, Ettore and Musco, Enzo. *Delitti contro l'ordine costituzione*. Bologna: Patron, 1984.

Ghini, Celso. *Il terremoto del 15 Giugno*. Milan: Feltrinelli, 1976.

Grevi, Vittorio. "Sistema penale dell'emergenza: la risposta legislativa al terrorismo." Gianfranco Pasquino (ed.) *La prova delle armi*. Bologna: Il Mulino, 1984.

Guerra, Patrizia and Revelli, Marco. "Bibliografia essenziale per la conoscenza della nuova destra italiana." Guido Quazza (ed.) *Fascismo oggi: nuova destra e cultura reazionaria negli anni ottanta*. Cuneo: Istituto Storico della Resistenza, 1983.

Guerri, Giordano Bruno. *Patrizio Peci: io l'infame*. Milan: Mondadori, 1983.

Guidorossi, Giovanna. *Gli Italiani e la politica*. Milan: Franco Angelli editore, 1984.

Gurr, Ted. *Why Men Rebel*. Princeton, N.J.: Princeton University Press, 1970.

Guzzanti, Paolo. *Il neofascismo e le sue organizzioni paramilitari*. Rome: PSI, 1973.

Hoffman, Bruce. *Right-Wing Terrorism in Europe*. Santa Monica, CA: Rand Corporation, 1982.

Hofstadter, Richard. *The Paranoid Style in American Politics.* New York: Vintage Books, 1967.

Jellamo, Ann. "J. Evola: il pensatore della tradizione." Franco Ferraresi (ed.) *La destra radicale.* Milan: Feltrinelli, 1984.

Kogan, Norman. *The Government of Italy.* New York: Thomas Crowell, 1962.

La Palombara, Joseph. "Italy: Fragmentation, Isolation and Alienation." Lucian Pye and Sidney Verba (eds.) *Political Culture and Political Development.* Princeton N.J.: Princeton University Press, 1965.

Laqueur, Walter. *Terrorism.* Boston: Little, Brown, 1977.

Laudi, Maurizio. *I casi di non punibilita dei terroristi "pentiti".* Varese: Giuffre editore, 1983.

Lazzero, Ricciotti. *La decima mas.* Milan: Rizzoli, 1984.

Linz, Juan. *Crisis, Breakdown, and Reequilibration.* Baltimore: The Johns Hopkins University Press, 1978.

Lipset, Seymour Martin and Raab, Earl. *The Politics of Unreason.* New York: Harper & Row, 1970.

Lorenzon, Guido. *Teste a carico.* Milan: Mondadori, 1976.

Mafai, Miriam. *L'uomo che sognava la lotta armata.* Milan: Rizzoli editore, 1984.

Majocchi, Luigi (ed.) *Rapporto sulla violenza fascista in Lombardia.* Rome: Cooperativa scrittori, 1975.

Manzini, Giorgio. *Indagine su un brigatista rosso.* Turin: Einaudi, 1978.

Marletti, Carlo. "Immagine, pubblivitte e ideologia del terrorismo." Luigi Bonante (ed.) *Dimensioni del terrorismo politico.* Milan: Angelli editore, 1979.

_____ . "Terrorismo e communizazione di massa." Gianfranco Pasquino (ed.) *La prova delle armi.* Bologna: Il Mulino, 1984.

Masini, Pier Carlo. *Storia degli anarchici italiani nell epoca degli attentati.* Milan: Rizzoli editore, 1981.

Mauro, Ezio. *Novelli: vivera a Torino.* Rome: Riuniti, 1980.

Melucci, Alberto. *L'Invenzione el presente.* Bologna: Il Mulino, 1982.

Migliorino, Luigi. "L'Italia e il terrorismo internazionale." Luigi Bonante (ed.) *Dimensioni del terrorismo politico.* Milan: Angelli editore, 1979.

Monicelli, Mino. *La follia veneta.* Rome: Riuniti, 1981.

_____ . *L'Ultrasinistra in Italia, 1968–1978.* Bari: Laterza, 1978.

Murgia, Pier Giuseppe. *Ritorneremo.* Milan: Sugar edizioni, 1976.

Mussi, Fabio. *Zangheri: Bologna '77.* Rome: Riuniti, 1978.

Negri, Antonio. *Proletari e stato.* Milan: Feltrinelli, 1976.

_____ . *Crisi e organizzazione operaia.* Milan: Feltrinelli, 1976.

Nozza, Marco. "'Quex': spontaneismo o progetto nazional-rivoluzionario." Guido Quazza (ed.) *Fascismo oggi: nuova destra e cultura reazionaria negli anni ottanta.* Cuneo: Istituto della Resistenza, 1983.

Pannunzio, Sergio. *Diritto, forza e violenza.* Bologna: Biblioteca di studi sociali, 1921.

Pansa, Giampaolo. *Borghese mi ha detto.* Milan: Palazzi editore, 1971.

_____ . *Storie Italiane di violenza e terrorismo.* Rome: Laterza, 1980.

Papa, Emilio. *Il processo alle Brigate Rosse.* Turin: Giappichelli, 1979.

Pasquino, Gianfranco. "Differenze a somiglianze per una ricerca sul terrorismo italiano." Donatella della Porta and Gianfranco Pasquino (eds.) *Terrorismo e violenza politica.* Bologna: Il Mulino, 1983.

Pasquino, Gianfranco and della Porta, Donatella. "Interpretations of Italian Left-Wing Terrorism." Peter Merkl (ed.) *Political Violence and Terror*. Berkeley: University of California Press, 1986.

Penniman, Howard (ed.) *Italy at the Polls: 1979*. Washington D.C.: American Enterprise Institute, 1981.

_____. *Italy at the Polls: The Parliamentary Elections of 1976*. Washington, D.C.: American Enterprise Institute, 1977.

Pisano, Vittofranco. *A Study of the Restructured Italian Intelligence and Security Services*. Washington, D.C.: Library of Congress, 1978.

Plebe, Armando. *Il libretto della destra*. Milan: Edizione del Borghese, (1972)

Ranchey, Alberto. *Accade in Italia, 1968-1977*. Milan: Garzanti, 1977.

Regni, Marino. "Labor Unions Industrial Action and Politics." Peter Lange and Sidney Tarrow (eds.) *Italy in Transition*. London: Frank Cass & Co., Ltd., 1980.

Revelli, Marco. "La nuova destra." Franco Ferraresi (eds.) *La destra radicale*. Milan: Feltrinelli, 1984.

Rodota, Stefano. "La risposta dello stato al terrorismo." Gianfranco Pasquino (ed.) *La prova delle armi*. Bologna: Il Mulino, 1984.

Rosenbaum, Petra. *Il nuovo fascismo*. Milan: Feltrinelli, 1975.

Russell, Charles and Miller, Bowman. "Profile of a Terrorist." Lawrence Freedman and Yonah Alexander (eds.) *Perspectives in Terrorism*. Wilmington Del.: Scholarly Resources, 1983.

Salierno, Giulio. *Autobiografia di un picchiatore fascista*. Turin: Einaudi editore, 1976.

Sassone, Marco. *La politica delle strage*. Padua: Marsilio, 1972.

Scarpati, Giancarlo. "La vicenda del '7 aprile'" Magistratura Democratica (eds.) *La magistratura di fronte al terrorismo e all eversione di sinistra*. Milan: Franco Angelli editore, 1982.

Schmid, Alex. *Political Terrorism*. New Brunswick, N.J.: Transaction Books, 1983.

Secchia, Pietro. *Lotta antifascista e giovani generazioni*. Milan: La Pietra, 1973.

Silj, Alessandro. *Never Again Without a Rifle*. New York: Harz Publishers, 1979.

Smith, Colin. *Carlos: Portrait of a Terrorist*. New York: Holt, Rinehart and Winston, 1976.

Smith, Denis Mack. *Mussolini*. New York: Vintage Books, 1982.

Soccorso Rosso (eds.) *Brigate Rosse*. Milan: Feltrinelli, 1976.

Soccorso Rosso Napolitano (eds.) *I NAP: Storia dei nuclei armati proletari*. Milan: Collectivo editoriale Libri Rossi, 1976.

Sossi, Mario. *Nella prigione delle BR*. Milan: Editoriale Nuova, 1979.

Sterling, Claire. *The Terror Network*. New York: Holt, Rinehart & Winston, 1981.

_____. *The Time of the Assassins*. New York: Holt, Rinehart & Winston, 1983.

Straiano, Corrado. *L Italia Nichilista*. Milan: Mondadori editore, 1982.

Strickland, D.A. and Krauss, Peter P. "Political Disintegration and Latent Terror." Michael Stohl (ed.) *The Politics of Terrorism*, 2nd ed. New York: Marcel Dekker, Inc., 1983.

Tedeschi, Mario. *Destra nazionale*. Rome: Edizioni del Borghese, 1972.

Tessadori, Vincenzo. *BR: Imputazione banda armata*. Milan: Garzanti, 1977.

Tilly, Charles, Tilly, Louise and Tilly, Richard. *The Rebellious Century*. Cambridge, Mass.: Harvard University Press, 1975.

Turone, Sergio. *Storia del sindaco in Italia.* Bari: Laterza, 1975.

Vanni, Renzo. *Trent'anni di regime bianco.* Pisa: Giardini editori, 1976.

Ventura, Angelo. "Il problema delle origine del terrorismo di sinistra." Donatella della Porta (ed.) *Terrorismo in Italia.* Bologna: Il Mulino, 1984.

Verni, Giovanni. *Dalla resistenza ad oggi.* Rome: edizioni della lega per le autonomie e i poteri locali, 1975.

Vettori, Giuseppe (ed.) *La sinistra extraparlamentare in Italia.* Rome: Newton Compton, 1973.

Vigna, Pier Luigi. *La finalita di terrorismo ed eversione.* Varese: Giuffre editore, 1981.

Weinberg, Leonard. *After Mussolini.* Washington D.C.: University Press of America, 1979.

Woodcock, George. *Anarchism.* New York: Meridian Books, 1962.

Wortman, Douglas. "The Christian Democrats: Masters of Survival." Penniman (ed.) *Italy at the Polls, 1979.*

Zangrandi, Ruggiero. *Inchiesta sul SIFAR.* Rome: Editori Riuniti, 1970.

Articles and Periodicals

Aldo Amoretti. "Risultati e problemi del tesseramento e del finanziamento del sindicato," *Rassegna Sindicale Quaderno* 12:50 (1974), pp. 55–57.

Almanaco PCI '76. Rome: PCI, 1976.

Tina Anselmi. "Il complotto di Licio Gelli: relazioni di Tina Anselmi, presidente della commissione parlamentare sulla P2." Supplement to *L'Espresso,* May 20, 1984.

Vittorio Berraccetti. "Aspetti e problemi del terrorismo di destra," *Questione Giustizia* 2:4 (1983), pp. 870–871.

Giancarlo Capaldo et al. "L'Eversione di destra a Roma dall'77 ad oggi: spunti per una ricostruzione del fenomeno," *Questione Giustizia* 2:4 (1983), pp. 939–948.

Franco Coppola. "Bologna 4 ergastioli per l'omicidio Amato," *La Repubblica,* April 6, 1984, p. 12.

Corriere della Sera. 1982.

Franco Ferrarese. "Radiografia del fascismo romano," *Rinascita* 29:11 (1972), pp. 18–20.

_____ . "I referimento teorico-dottrinali della destra radicale," *Questione Giustizia* 11:4 (1983), pp. 881–892.

Claudio Gerino. "Ora stiamo braccando latitanti dei NAR," *La Repubblica,* October 7, 1982, p. 10.

Daniele Mastrogiacomo. "Autonomia, 7 secoli di carcere," *La Repubblica,* April 16, 1984, p. 5.

Nazareno Pagani and Matteo Spina. "Quel giovedi di paura," *Panorama* 26:623 (March, 1978), pp. 38–43.

Carlo Rossella. "Sapore di golpe," *Panorama* 25:573 (April, 1977), pp. 42–44.

La Repubblica. 1976–1984.

Giancarlo Scarpati. "Il processo per la strage dell' 'Italicus," *Questione Giustizia* 2:4 (1983), pp. 893–911.

Thomas Sheehan. "Italy: Behind the Ski Mask," *The New York Review of Books* 26:13 (August, 1959), p. 21.

————. "Italy: Terror on the Right," *The New York Review of Books* 27:21 (1981), pp. 23–26.

La Stampa. 1970–1982

Partito Comunista Italiano 1981. Rome: PCI, 1981.

Pier Luigi Vigna, L"'Omicidio del Magistrato Vittorio Occorsio: i processi e alcuni riflessioni," *Questione Giustizia* 2:4 (1983), pp. 913–933.

Public Documents

Italy. Francesco Amato, Giudice Istruttore. *Ordinanza/Sentenza* N 10067/79. Tribunale di Roma, Uffizio Istruzione.

Ordinanza/sentenza N 1027/79. Tribunale di Roma, Uffizio Istruziore.

Ordinanza/Sentenza N 1067/69. Tribunale di Roma, Uffizio Istruzione.

Annuario Statistico Italiano, 1975 and 1983 editions. Rome: Istituto Centrale di Statistica.

Annuario di Statistiche Provinciali Vol. 12., Rome: Istituto Centrale di Statistica.

Atti Parlamentari. V Legislatura. Senato della Repubblica. Sedita 416, February 1971.

Atti Parlamentari 22. V Legislatura. Seduta 420.

La corte di assise di appello di Firenze. *Sentenza* November 11, 1977, April 9, 1976 and December 12, 1978.

Corte D'Assise d'appello di Milano. *Sentenza* N 7/80.

Sentenza N 70/80.

Corte d'Assise di Roma. *Sentenza* 2/83.

Sentenza 31/81 RG.

Corte D'Assise D'Appello di Torino. *Sentenza* N2/83.

Corte D'Assise di Torino. *Sentenza* N17/81.

Sentenza N 17/82.

Corte di Firenze. *Sentenza.* April 4, 1983.

Luigi Gennaro, Giudice Istruttore. *Ordinanza/Sentenza* N 2736/80A. Tribunale di Roma. N/5686/80A.

Giudice Istruttori, Tribunale Civile e Penale di Milano. *Sentenza/Ordinanza* 23/82.

Giudice Instruttore. *Ordinanza* N223/81. Tribunale civile e penale di Milano.

Giudice Istruttore. *Sentenza/ordinanza* 231/83. Tribunale civile e penale di Milano.

Giudice Istruttore. *Ordinanza/Sentenza* 490/81F. Tribunale civile e penale di Milano.

Ferdinando Imposimato Giudice Istruttore. *Ordinanza/Sentenza* N54/80A. Tribunale di Roma.

Publicco Misistero. *Requisitoria* N. 921/80F. Procura della Repubblica in Milano.

Relazioni della Commissione Parlamentare D'Inchiesta sull Strage di Via Fani. Rome: Tipografia del Senato, 1983.

Relazioni di minoranza della commissione parlamentare d'inchiesta sulla strage di via Fani sul sequestro e l'assassaino di Aldo Moro e sul terrorismo in Italia. Rome: Tipografia del Senato, 1983.

U.S. Terrorism and Security: The Italian Experience. Report of the Subcommittee on Security and Terrorism of the Committee on the Judiciary, United States Senate. Washington, D.C.: U.S. Government Printing Office, 1984.

Reports

Gian Carlo Caselli and Donatella della Porta. *Per una storia del terrorismo di sinistra.* Report delivered at the Istituto Cattaneo Conference on Political Violence and Terrorism in Italy, Bologna, April 29–30 1983.

Gianfranco Pasquino and Donatella della Porta. *Interpretations of Italian Left-Wing Terrorism.* Paper, XII World Congress of the International Political Science Association, Rio de Janeiro, August 9–14, 1982.

Unpublished Material

Luciana Stortoni. "Analisi di una organizzazione terrorista: Prima Linea." Tesi di laurea, Political Science faculty, University of Florence, 1983.

Interviews

Interview with Judge Marcello De Roberto, Florence, April 6, 1984.

Interview with Dott, Pier Luigi Vigna, Sostituto procuratore della repubblica, Florence, April 1984.

Interview with Frederick Vreeland, political counselor at the U.S. Embassy in Rome, June 1984.

INDEX